Fruit TREES

in SMALL SPACES

Abundant Harvests from Your Own Backyard

Colby Eierman

with photos by Erin Kunkel
and recipes by Mike Emanuel

Timber Press
Portland | London

Published in 2012 by Timber Press, Inc.

The Haseltine Building
133 S.W. Second Avenue, Suite 450
Portland, Oregon 97204-3527
timberpress.com

2 The Quadrant
135 Salusbury Road
London NW6 6RJ
timberpress.co.uk

Printed in China

Library of Congress Cataloging-in-Publication Data

Eierman, Colby.
    Fruit trees in small spaces: abundant harvests from your own backyard/Colby
Eierman; with photos by Erin Kunkel.—1st ed.
        p. cm.
    Includes bibliographical references and index.
    ISBN 978-1-60469-190-0
    1. Fruit trees. 2. Fruit. 3. Backyard gardens. 4. Orchards. I. Title. II. Title:
Abundant harvests from your own backyard.
    SB355.E42 2012
    634—dc23   2011042489

Catalog records for this book are available from the British Library.

Contents

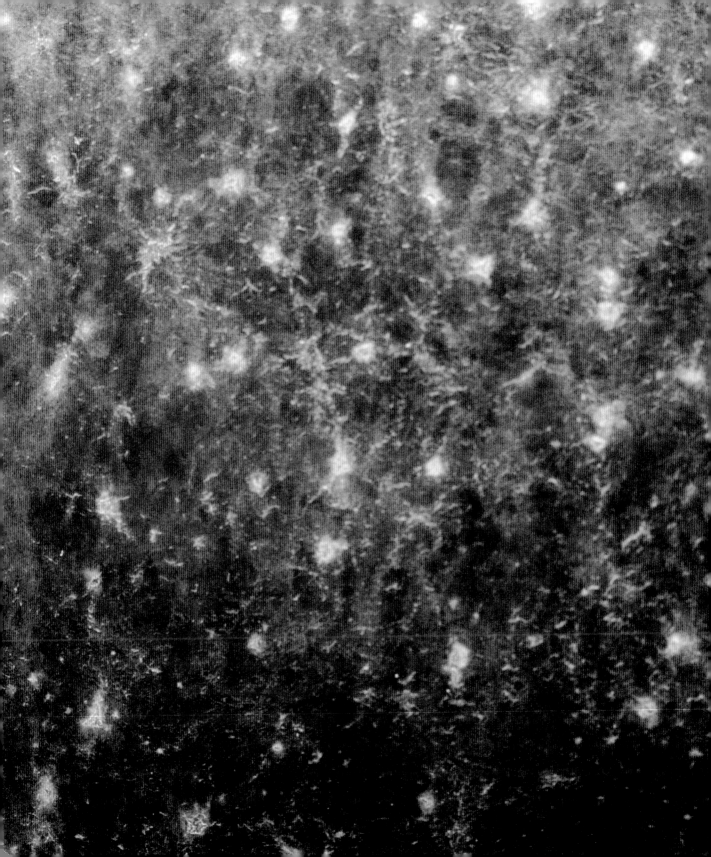

Foreword

by Rosalind Creasy

I first met Colby in the magnificent garden at COPIA, which was known for its dedication to understanding and celebrating American food, wine, and arts. It was 2004 and I was there to photograph fruit trees. The gardens were beautiful, the fruit trees were in a unique landscaped setting, and I needed photographs to offer inspiration for home gardeners for my book *Edible Landscaping*.

Everything was so well grown and there were so many unusual things that I sought out the gardener to learn more. Most of the trees were small, with many of them in containers—so appropriate for the home gardener. There was an espaliered quince, something I'd never seen before. Apples, plums, cherries, and peaches along with different citrus were planted in stop-you-in-your-tracks rusted containers. There were 3-in-1 plantings, a fabulous way to grow a variety of fruits in a small space. It was a luxury to see so many fruits in one place at one time, and to see so many ideas for growing these fruits in a small space.

After 30 years of experience as a landscape designer, I knew that most people want smaller fruit trees for any number of reasons: size of yards, limited time, and the desire to have a wide variety of fruits rather than one single fruit tree that dominates the yard and overwhelms the gardener with a surplus of fruit. Unfortunately, for decades now, most of the information on growing fruit trees, both in books and online, has been aimed at people who are maintaining single-crop orchards.

This book, on the other hand, focuses on growing multiple orchard fruits as part of the landscape in today's smaller gardens. Home gardeners will find they can grow the fruit they love, and plenty of it, even if their yards are small. Growing instructions include selected information for different climates and conditions. Colby's experience with the trees themselves and the techniques required to grow them in a smaller space means that he is also a master pruner. He understands how to grow and prune trees for the best looks and highest fruit production. With this book, he brings this knowledge and expertise to help home gardeners get the best from their trees.

To round out the book, there are the recipes. Cookbooks generally overlook homegrown fruits, and yet that's where the treasure is. Sadly, most home gardeners, even when they grow some of their own fruit, don't know how to harvest at the peak of perfection. Colby guides us through this critical step, and then takes it a giant step further by giving us both time-honored recipes, such as poached pears and fruit jams and leathers, and going way beyond with new approaches.

Even with my years of experience, I discovered new techniques. When the apple tree is in full harvest, I no longer have to rely on applesauce to take care of the overflow. With the recipes in this imaginative collection, I now can branch out from applesauce to make apple chips or get past apple pie with just solo apples and add other fruits on a crunchy galette base. Who knew that peach leaves could be used to flavor wine or that gardeners in cold climates, whose container-grown lemon might not produce much in the way of fruit, can take full advantage of their plants by harvesting their leaves to make an incredible syrup to be used as part of a spritzer or brushed between the layers of a lemon chiffon cake?

Most of all, this book is a great primer, easy to use, and easy to understand. It demonstrates that growing fruit trees need not be a daunting task, with reliable information based on experience and with an emphasis on organic growing. Soon you'll be showing off your heirloom apples or latest variety of pluot, introducing friends to the unique taste of the kumquat, taking the plunge and learning to make a true fruit jam, or harvesting peach leaves to see just what they add to wine.

Acknowledgments

I must start with a short word of gratitude to my family, who make everything worthwhile. Thanks first to my wife, Megan, who knew I wanted to see this book through and provided the time and encouragement for me to do that. And to my sons, Peter and Henry, thank you so much for being patient and for not spilling anything on my computer.

This book has been nothing if not a collective effort, and working on it has reinforced my belief that generosity and collaboration are qualities to be cherished, cultivated, and sought out in all endeavors. All the folks involved have brought an enthusiastic spirit in contributing to this common and simple notion: that it is good, beautiful, delicious, and fun to grow some of our own fruit at home.

This book would not exist without the steady research and writing support of Marianne Lipanovich. I am endlessly grateful for her keen sensibilities and solid plant knowledge. Marianne's bright and easy-going way comes through in Part Two of this book.

For good reason, Erin Kunkel is one of the most sought-after photographers in the San Francisco Bay Area and beyond. She was the first person I thought of for this project and I am so glad she was willing to sign on. Erin knows plants and brings an artist's eye to even the most pragmatic shot. The calm and steady way in which she works was a welcome and inspiring part of this process.

Chef Mike Emanuel brought the recipe section of this book into fruition with a collection of recipes that help bring out and/or preserve the best of homegrown fruit. Mike and his wife, Jenny, are the consummate hosts, and their cooking always takes advantage of the best the season has to offer. I am so thankful for their friendship and contribution to this book.

Mike Tomlinson of Dave Wilson Nursery generously provided photographs of specific fruit varieties. Pattiann Koury and Aya Brackett kindly supplied photographs that helped to make the text visually complete.

Richi Meecham and Degge Hays both bigheartedly opened up their gardens for us to photograph and explore. Degge has also been my trusted council on pruning, variety selection, and most any garden topic that comes to mind. Ed Laivo of Devil Mountain Nursery offered his reflections on backyard orchard culture and has, over the years, been a fountain of fruit tree knowledge.

Steve Sando of Rancho Gordo New World Specialty Foods introduced me to the folks at Timber Press and helped me navigate the process. Many days his beans also helped to sustain my work.

I would like to thank Rosalind Creasy for contributing the foreword to this book and, more importantly, for forging a path for folks like myself who are now able to make their living doing "edible landscaping." That term was coined with the introduction of her seminal 1982 book, *Complete Book of Edible Landscaping*.

And thanks to the folks who have helped my development as a gardener.

When I was 15 years old, Janet Sanchez provided the seeds, compost, and encouragement to start a garden with her son, Ramon. Thanks to my mom, for reminding us that it was expensive to pump all that water and we had better have something to eat at the end of it all. Thanks to my dad, for encouraging me in so many ways to do things with passion and for steering me toward landscape architecture.

I have had the great privilege to work under and alongside some brilliant teachers over the years. When I was a freshman in the University of Oregon's Urban Farm class, Richard Britz laid out a vision for urban food production that has informed much of my work since. If you find a copy of his out-of-print book,

The Edible City Resource Manual, pick it up. Also at the U of O, Professor Ann Bettman let me know that edible landscaping was something that could be done artfully and to the great benefit of a city's inhabitants.

Every year, Orin Martin, manager of the Alan Chadwick Garden at University of California, Santa Cruz, shares his passion for apples (and garlic, peppers, roses and many other things) to a new crop of apprentices. It was an eye-opening experience to be part of the 1999 vintage, and I think often of his lectures on the chalet porch.

Jeff Dawson is a household name among gardeners in the California wine country. I spent an extremely formative and informative year as Jeff's assistant in the gardens of COPIA, the now defunct food and wine destination in Napa, California. His generosity and tutelage that year and since have offered profound insights into the dynamic life of garden systems.

My boys don't actually care where their food comes from, as long as it is coated in freshly whipped cream.

Preface

I grew up in Sonoma County, California. When I was 15 years old, my best friend, Ramon, and I got the idea that we should plant a garden. Though I am hesitant to admit it now, I think it had something to do with how much we were listening to Crosby, Stills, Nash, and Young's version of Joni Mitchell's hippie anthem, "Woodstock." Perhaps we took a little too literally the line, "We've got to get ourselves back to the garden." Ramon's mom, a garden writer, was quick to offer up all the compost, seeds, plant divisions, and advice we wanted, and before long our garden was a place for friends to work, eat, and hang out. We would cook hot dogs and s'mores over a small fire pit and roll out our sleeping bags between garden rows after a good day's work. In many ways, Ramon and I have been trying to get ourselves back to that garden ever since.

I took away something important from that first experience of planting a garden with my friends and sharing the harvest. Growing food gave me a chance to share something essential, and that is the reason I have put growing food at the core (to get started with the fruit metaphors) of my life's study and work.

Speaking of study, it was my dad who first suggested that I consider landscape architecture as a possible future profession. Ramon and I had started the garden, and I was taking drafting as an elective in high school. Pops had the foresight to introduce me to a family friend who was a landscape architect in the neighboring town of Petaluma, and I started working in her office. I eventually found myself studying landscape architecture at the University of Oregon and made a second home in the urban farm run by the department. Not every professor embraced my desire to include edibles in absolutely every single one of my design exercises, but it was pretty clear that I had found a good place to study.

Although I was just starting high school when I was first bitten by the gardening bug, it wasn't until I moved from California to Oregon that I started planting fruit trees. I recently reviewed the weather data for the winter of 1995–96 in Eugene, and nearly every day had at least a bit of rain. Kind of unfortunate that this was the winter I would get inspired to work with fruit trees, but you can't question fate. I started the season with bright, shiny yellow raingear (hat and all) like that modeled on a box of Gorton's frozen fish sticks. By the time the ground dried out, sometime in July, the extremities of that suit were stained with the sticky Willamette Valley clay soil, and I had taken a leap in my experience as a gardener.

Planting a fruit tree feels optimistic and kind. Every year, as planting season approaches, I am charged with anticipation for the opportunity to try out a new variety, pruning technique, or training method. The obvious reason to plant a fruit tree is so that you can eat delicious homegrown fruit. But I prefer to take a broader assessment of my own success in the orchard. Have I enjoyed my time getting to know these trees? Have I shared a meal with my friends in that space? Do my kids know where their food comes from? Sure, these are broad concepts, but from this vantage point the occasional crop failure ends up being easier to swallow, even if there's nothin' to chew.

In the years since college, I've earned a living exclusively by designing and caring for edible landscapes. I have planted, tended, harvested, and eaten quite a bit of fruit in that time and cannot seem to propose a design to one of my clients that doesn't include at least one fruit tree in the scheme. More commonly, a mix of perennial fruit forms the bones of the spaces I design. Likewise, the homes that I've owned or rented have all been left more fruitful, and although I might miss the harvest, I don't regret the investment.

I am deeply grateful to the folks who helped me learn about growing food, especially when I was younger, and I hope you might do the same for a young person. My path was made easier thanks to folks such as Rosalind Creasy, who helped break food crops out of the potager.

Our diets and our food system are ripe (get it?) for an overhaul, and squeezing more good food into our urban and suburban yards seems like a great start to me. In this book, I try to share some of my ideas on how to be successful growing fruit trees in small spaces. I'll tip my hand and tell you right now that the best idea I have come across is to make fruit trees part of your life in the same way you would a good friend.

Introduction

"Aaaahhh, that is amazing! I've never tasted a pluot!" These are the kind of things a gardener loves to hear. As anyone whohas toiled to nurture a struggling fruit tree and enjoyed even the smallest harvest can attest, growing your own fruit is a uniquely satisfying experience. Many small urban or suburban lots offer plenty of space for planting and growing food. Quite often, planting a small vegetable garden is just the beginning, as we eventually realize that adding perennial fruit trees can provide a big return on a small investment. And even if you don't own any dirt, you can grow a dwarf lemon or an espaliered apple in a container.

No space is too small to include fruit trees.

This book is designed to help you successfully grow fruit trees in small spaces. That small space could be your entire backyard, a row of espalier along a fence, a few containers in a corner of your patio, or all of the above. You can make use of many tree planting options around your home, school, and/or business, and my goal is help you enjoy that process.

Our story opens with an introduction to the fruit-growing year. Trees, like mothers, require regular visits to be happy, and the first part of this book will guide you through a full calendar's worth of care, from planting the tree to harvesting the fruit and end-of-year cleanup.

Next, you'll read about some important design decisions that will set you up for tasty garden triumphs. Before you begin planting, consider the features of your space, such as your area's macro and microclimate and the hardiness zone in your area. What other features will share the space with fruit trees? A chicken coop, lawn, path, patio, and a wood-fired oven are a few options to consider. I'll offer a few case studies and drawings that show some ideas for including fruit trees in a garden.

Part Two introduces the fruit tree family album, with nearly 300 different fruit varieties available to the small space fruit grower. You'll learn about choosing plants, rootstocks, and three major fruit groups: stone fruits, pome fruits, and citrus. This is followed by some in-depth recommendations about how to meet your chosen tree's every need, from planting, to pruning, to pest control, fertilizing, and beyond.

Part Three covers orchard planning and care, including a variety of soil amendments and cover crops, instructions for planting in ground and in containers, irrigation considerations, how to deal with pests and diseases, and pruning and training methods.

Finally, the recipes in Part Four offer many ideas on what the heck to do with all of this delicious fruit. These recipes are written with the home gardener in mind—because, after all, this is what the book is all about.

Depending on where you garden and the types of fruits you grow, you'll encounter an abundance of challenges and enjoy many sweet surprises when you grow a variety of fruit. Reading this book should give you a good idea of which fruits will thrive in your area and will help you enjoy keeping them healthy and productive.

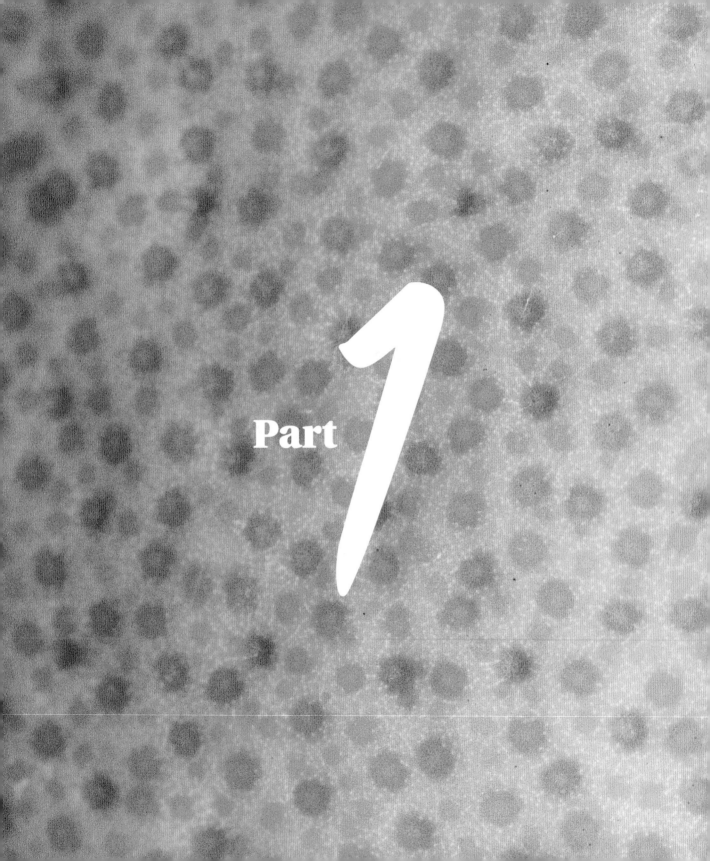

Part 1

Home Orchard Primer:
Designing the Orchard Life

A Year in the Orchard

Growing fruit is a year-round activity, and each step in the process is important for success. Each step also represents an opportunity to make a connection, be it with nature, friends and family, or ourselves. Caring for my trees is one of the ways that my time in the garden has at the very least made me a better gardener and perhaps a better person. Although taking care of trees can sometimes seem like just another bullet point on an already full to-do list, my time pruning or spreading mulch usually feels more like a break from other chores. If I am lucky, that perspective translates to the rest of my life, and I can bring that gardener's mindset to folding laundry or whatever is called for at the moment.

Just so everyone is totally clear about what you are getting your-selves into (in this book and in your yard), I'll start with some high-lights of a single year in the home orchard. I don't want you calling me up saying, "Hey, you never told me I had to prune these things!" I am also laying this out at the start to emphasize the importance of good planning and design to the overall success of your tree fruit growing endeavors. One important point cannot be overstated: the right plant, planted with care in a choice location, takes you 90 percent of the way toward having something tasty to eat.

This chapter will lead you through the most important activities you can undertake in a year to keep your trees healthy and to ensure that your foray into fruit growing is a pleasurable one. This material is the first step in an exercise that answers the big questions: What should I plant, and how do I take care of it? By understanding the rhythms and responsibilities of a year in the orchard, you can anticipate challenges before they arise and also create a plan for how your life will blend with the life of your trees. (For example, if you take a vacation every summer, you probably shouldn't plant a lot of midseason peach trees that ripen while you are away.) If you follow this outline, making adjustments to fit your specific garden and region, fruit growing will be a delicious adventure.

If you have yet to start your home orchard, you are on already on the right track. You are looking at books about fruit trees (this one, and maybe a few others) and learning about such essentials as varieties, pruning, and chill hours (the average number of hours that your dormant trees will spend "chilling" below 45°F).

A front yard apple espalier makes a great light fence, with room for more plants underneath.

Designing, Selecting Varieties, and Preparing the Soil

Your goal in this first year is to align three important decisions: Decide what you want to grow, what you can grow, and what kind of system will support it all. Don't get bogged down at this stage. Gardens are living, breathing, and ever-changing. If something isn't quite right, you can (and should) change it later. Just plant something!

It pays to plan ahead, whether you are designing a suburban lot with a few fruit trees; building a new patio, a wood-fired oven, or an arbor; or simply adding a few potted citrus to your deck. Take time to prepare: plant cover crops, choose pots, and design watering systems so that your collection of trees can thrive as a beautiful, living orchard.

Planting a 'Nagami' kumquat (*Citrus kumquat* 'Nagami') in a pot

Planting, Replanting, and Repotting

If you're gardening in a mild climate, you can often find a good selection of dormant, bare-root fruit trees in the winter at local nurseries. Try to find out when the nursery will receive its first shipment of trees to get the pick of the litter. Many specialty nurseries will let you know what is coming or even bring in a specific variety that you know you want. I encourage you to get to know the folks at your local nursery, because they can be an amazing resource for what works and what doesn't in your area. Mail order can also be an excellent option, especially if you are ordering several trees, don't have a local nursery, or are searching for something a little more obscure.

If you are buying potted trees (still a good option), this step will happen a little later in the season. If you missed the dormant season and want to buy a potted tree, many nurseries will pot up whatever bare-root trees they don't sell in the winter and make those availably in early summer, after they are well-rooted. The selection generally won't be as good as winter choices, but this might be your best option, depending on your schedule. When planting a dormant tree in the ground or in a pot, do some initial light pruning to get things growing in a way that best fits your space.

Boo! Dwarf citrus is easy to cover and will benefit from being covered when temperatures get too cold.

Protecting Plants from Weather Extremes

The interval between tree planting and those first pink buds swelling and bursting into leaf and flower can be a cautious time for the freshly minted home orchardist. If you are anything like me or other gardeners I know, you will at some point be tempted by a plant that is considered "marginal" for your area. This means that in some years, the plant will be ready to grow before the weather has decided to stay consistently above freezing temperatures (32°F). Before you buy, consider whether you are willing to move pots around, string lights around the plants for warmth, and drape frost blankets over them to protect tender selections from spring frosts. Depending on the setting, I usually recommend that folks start out planting the proven performers before trying the more marginal selections. I am fortunate to live in an area where a long list of worthy replacements are ready to step in if one of the trees in my mini-orchard turns out to be too tender for Napa's relatively mild weather.

Heavy rains early in the season can also wreak havoc with fruit trees. It is heartbreaking to see a plum in full flower quickly brought down a peg by Mother Nature. Draping the trees in frost blankets can help soften the blow of falling raindrops, and the microclimate they create can still be attractive to passing pollinators, which are necessary for fruit set.

Thinning the Fruit

It's a tough thing to do, walking up to a tree that is doing just what you've asked of it—setting an abundant crop of fruit—and stripping much of that potential harvest from its tightly held stems. But fruit thinning is preferred over the alternative—letting the tree slip into an every-other-year fruiting cycle or letting it become so overburdened with fruit that the undersized fruit cannot ripen fully. The combination of not thinning aggressively enough and not staking up laden branches is a recipe for disaster in the form of broken branches. In general, if you can assess a branch's ability to support the amount of fruit that is trying to be set and then thin to that standard, you will do the tree, and yourself, a great service. Start early, when the fruit is around nickel-sized, and the task should be pretty easy, depending on how many trees need attention from your nimble, soon-to-be-numb, fingers. A good rule is to leave 4 to 6 inches between fruits.

This will happen only a few times before "thin early and often" becomes your mantra.

Providing Water

Water can be delivered to your plants via any number of methods. Some folks prefer to water by hand with a wand, or they create a depression in the soil around the tree and let a hose fill that up as they tend other parts of the garden. If you use an irrigation system, it is a good idea to run a test before you really need to use it. Drip lines get damaged, sprinkler heads pop off or are colonized by spiders, and general degradation sets in over the months between watering cycles.

Of course, plants in pots and containers will need the most attention as far as water is concerned. I will take this opportunity to remind you of the benefits of choosing the largest pot that makes sense for the space you have. Soil in a large container doesn't heat up as fast as it would in a smaller pot, and larger containers offer the obvious advantage of more root space and more water holding capacity.

Depending on soil type and tree size, specimens planted in the ground will benefit from less frequent irrigation (a week or longer between watering) for longer duration (30 minutes plus). A general rule is to allow the top ½ inch of soil to dry between watering cycles.

Microsprinklers can be an excellent choice for watering your trees.

Maintaining and Pruning Trees in Summer

Summer pruning is one of the most important tasks for maintaining fruit trees in a small space. A fruit tree puts significant stored resources into creating leaves, which collect solar energy and convert that into carbohydrates to support its growth. By removing some of those leaves midseason, before they've had a chance to collect a full season's worth of sunshine, you can effectively limit the size of the tree.

Many gardeners find summer pruning quite satisfying, and not just because the weather is usually nice. Unlike dormant pruning that you undertake in the winter, in the summer you don't have to imagine what the tree will look like after it leafs out. You have the benefit of seeing where light is actually hitting the leaves and the overall shape of the tree.

By midsummer, the fruit is getting heavier, and some branches are surely feeling the strain. Take a cue from the commercial orchards and provide some staking or tying to support the ripening crop. A handy branch support can be made by cutting a V into one end of a piece of 1-by-4 lumber.

POLLINATOR VERSUS POLLINIZER

The terms *pollinator* and *pollinizer* are often confused. The pollinator is the vector (insect or bird) that moves the pollen from flower to flower. The pollinizer is the plant whose flowers serve as the pollen source for another plant's flowers. A good pollinizer provides compatible, viable, and plentiful pollen and blooms at the same time as the plant that needs to be pollinated. Many fruit trees require that flowers be pollinated to set fruit. Some trees are self-pollinated, or self-fruitful, which means the flowers on the tree can pollinate themselves or other flowers on the same tree. Other trees require pollination from flowers on a separate tree to produce fruit. Pollination requires pollinators, such as flies, bees, moths, or birds, that move the pollen from blossom to blossom.

My buddy Richi makes some choice summer cuts on this young plum.

Sitting in the orchard, having a drink

Some trees that are particularly susceptible to fungal attack, such as apricots, are best pruned when the weather is dry. If you garden in an area with dry summers and wet winters, prune your apricots a month before the expected first rains.

Relaxing in Your Orchard

I'm sure I don't need to remind you about this, but I do want to reinforce the idea that a home orchard isn't just about producing tasty fruit. Complementary plantings of herbs, vegetables, and flowers can enhance the feeling and functionality of your little orchard. It can be a place for quiet reflection, raucous parties, or both. If you are still in the design stage, think about how your orchard can support other things you like, in addition to fruit trees. I love being able to work with friends and family in the orchard and then sit in the shade and enjoy some food and drink. Make space for a bistro table, pizza oven, fire pit, or even a hot tub to help you to enjoy the beautiful place you created. Lights hung in your trees can serve the dual purpose of creating ambiance and raising the ambient temperature on particularly cool evenings.

Harvesting and Consuming the Crop

Whoo-hoo! Harvest time is here! You've watched as the tender flower buds emerged and worried as that late spring rain knocked some of those precious petals to the ground. Despite the challenges this vintage has (surely) presented, your trees managed to set some quantity of fruit, and now it is turning color and starting to look ready to eat. Right about now, you might have a couple questions: how to tell when to pick your fruit, and the happy question of what to do with all this fruit. Sometimes, answering the latter will help answer the former, and the recipes included in this book should help with that. Assessing ripeness in fruit is not an altogether unpleasant task, because it mostly consists of tasting it. If the flavor is good, but sugars seem to be low, that fruit might be a good candidate for use in a recipe that calls for adding sugar.

I say, if it's hanging into
your yard, you get to eat it.

A fresh load of mulch can do wonders for the look and health of your trees.

Spreading compost around a backyard apricot

Cleaning Up

If part of your goal is to have healthy trees that don't require much in the way of spraying for pests and disease (duh), cleanup is perhaps the most important step after variety selection. Some fruit is going to fall on the ground. This is part of a fruit tree's natural rhythm, and you would be wise to pick up dropped fruit in a timely fashion. Rotting fruit isn't an aroma many people list as a favorite, but, on the contrary, pests and diseases love it, and fallen fruit is a perfect overwintering site for pests and diseases. I have found that tasks such as pruning, raking, weeding, and mulching contribute to healthier plants and will save you time, money, and hassle related to pest and disease control. You should also make sure that whatever mulch or ground cover you have chosen isn't creeping too close to the trunk of your tree; the moisture that is held in the material can encourage disease if it is allowed to touch the bark, so keep mulch about 3 inches away from the base of the tree.

Feeding and Caring for the Soil

Even if your trees are growing in pots, they are taking in nearly all of their nutrition through the roots in the soil. If that soil is also living—that is, biologically active—those roots have more access to the air, water, and nutrients that the tree needs to, among other things, create new cells in the form of branches, leaves, and fruit. The fall is a great time to think about the biological activity in your soil. Whether you are sowing cover crops, mulching with finished compost, or brewing a batch of compost tea, fall is the best time. Mulching with chips from smaller (pencil-sized branches) of deciduous trees, which have a carbon-to-nitrogen ratio that is thought to encourage beneficial fungal organisms in the soil, helps to break down nutrients and make them available to plants. Many other local sources of mulch and ground covers can also be effective in protecting the soil from weathering and compaction.

SPRAYING TREES

To be honest, I don't enjoy spraying my trees with much other than aerobically brewed compost tea, but that isn't always in the best interest of an abundant harvest and long-term tree health. Two types of sprays can be very helpful if you are struggling with insect or disease infestations. The first is horticultural oil for use in the dormant season (not to be confused with lime sulfur, sometimes called dormant oil) that smothers and kills the eggs and larvae of soft-bodied insects such as aphids, scale, caterpillars, and mites. Some newer oils can be plant-based and/or made in lighter solutions that are acceptable for use throughout the year.

The second type of spray is used to control or suppress fungal disease. Either lime sulfur or organic copper can be effective if application is timed correctly and the weather cooperates. These dormant sprays can be helpful, but keep in mind that sulfur will damage apricots, so choose copper to control fungal disease.

Spraying a dormant tree

Winter Pruning and Training

I have already lauded the benefits of summer pruning, but winter pruning is still an important task in the mini-orchard. In the dormant season, pruning cuts made in one- and even two-year-old growth, near the tip of the branch, tend be invigorating; they encourage a growth response in the coming season that will be longer than what was removed. Cuts closer to the trunk send the message to the branch that it has filled its required space and can stop growing right there. Peaches and nectarines set their fruit on young growth, so winter pruning can be a great tool to encourage new growth and fruit production.

You can train your trees to direct growth at most any time of the year, but I tend to do the bulk of it in the winter, when I can see the form of the tree and access the branches more easily. Spreaders, weights, and string are all useful tools for encouraging the tree to grow where you want it to go. If you are establishing an espalier or another trained form, winter pruning allows you to see the structure and set a good foundation. Winter is a also good time to cut some grafting stock and place it in the freezer for any topwork (grafting cut branches, or scions, of one variety of tree onto the branches of another tree) you might want to do next year.

Redirecting some growth on a cherry tree with pole pruners

GRAFTiNG

You might consider doing some grafting on your trees for a variety of reasons. Whether you need a second variety for pollination, you want to extend the harvest with a new variety, or you are unhappy with the variety you have and want something else, all grafting techniques seek to achieve one primary goal: to marry two different varieties of fruit onto a single tree.

Select and source your scion wood (the new variety that you will be adding to an existing tree) during the dormant season. Many garden groups host scion exchanges, which are also a great way to meet other fruit tree enthusiasts and pick their brains. Dormant sticks of scion wood can be kept in a well-sealed bag in the fridge, freezer, or root cellar. Wood can also be collected and grafted in the few weeks before bud break, eliminating the need to store the scion.

CLEFT GRAFTING

In the dormant season, select a branch or a rootstock 2–4 inches in diameter and make a clean, flat saw cut. With a grafting cleaver or large, sharp knife, split the branch or rootstock vertically, about 2–4 inches down from the saw cut. With a very sharp knife, cut the bottom few inches of two pieces of scion into narrow V shapes. Wedge open the cleft in the rootstock or larger branch with your grafting tool or a chisel, and do your best to line up the cambium layers (the thin layer of material just under the bark) between the branch/rootstock and the scion. Then seal all exposed cuts with grafter's paint. Cleft grafting can also be done with smaller, matching diameter branches and scions.

WHIP AND TONGUE GRAFTING

Whip grafting is a great way to add a new variety to an existing tree. In the dormant season, choose a branch that is the same diameter as the scion. With sharp pruners or a sharp knife, make a diagonal cut with about I inch of surface area on both the branch and the scion (so that they will fit together). Then cut a notch in the face of both cuts, about ½ inch long and about ¼ inch deep, with a "tongue" facing up on the branch and a "tongue" facing down on the scion. Fit the two pieces together at the notches (sliding the tongue of the scion into the notch made in the branch), matching the cambium layers, and wrap the joint with grafting tape.

The larger branch here was a root sucker that went unnoticed for a few years. A new cultivar is now being cleft grafted onto it.

Cleft grafting can work well on smaller, matching diameter branches and scions.

Preparing a scion for cleft grafting

Designing Your Small Orchard

You might find it a stretch to call your little slice of fruit-growing heaven a full-blown orchard, but what the heck, it's your place and you can do what you want. Personally, I like the images that the word *orchard* conjures up. I like thinking about the orchards that used to (and in some cases still do) dominate the landscapes where we live. I like old wooden fruit boxes and the smell of fermenting cider. I try to seek out the old-timers in my

Plant fruit trees in an accessible spot for easy picking.

community to tap into their hard-earned knowledge of how to keep critters at bay or to glean an old family recipe for applesauce.

I also want to be part of a different type of agricultural community that is striving to weave some of that not-so-distant past into our modern lives. Some of us are actually going to produce a large amount of what we consume from our own urban or suburban plots. Many of us will only dabble in growing and still find a valuable connection to our sustenance and perhaps our community. That is probably the main appeal for me in writing this book—to enhance someone's connection to his or her village through food production.

One of my favorite things about a garden is that it is never finished. It is always changing, growing and (not to get too morbid here at the start) at the same time dying. Some plants can thrive for a few years and then outgrow their space or simply stop prospering. Remind yourself of this fact as you begin designing your space and selecting trees. Plants aren't the Great Pyramids of Giza, after all. A garden is a living, breathing entity, and with simple tools, we can change the things that aren't working for us. We can provide all the food, water, and shelter a tree could want and it still might die on us. If and when that happens, remember that plenty of worthy candidates are in line right behind it, waiting to fill that space.

This chapter starts with a broad overview of the climatic factors that affect which trees will grow where you live. From here, we move to the finer details of your specific site and explore ways to take advantage of the complexities inherent is most garden plots. You could design your yard and your fruit trees in an infinite number of ways, but you have to choose only one design. A few of my favorite design elements are covered here, followed by three sample designs.

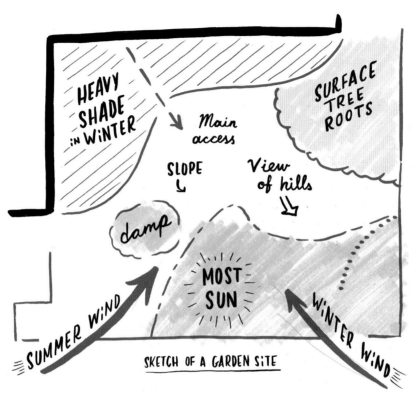

HEAVY SHADE in WiNTER

SURFACE TREE ROOTS

Main access

SLOPE

View of hills

damp

MOST SUN

SUMMER WIND

WINTER WIND

SKETCH OF A GARDEN SITE

Understanding Your Site

You probably already have a manila folder that is struggling to contain the growing number of inspirational images you've ripped out of magazines. But before you begin working on a design that includes all those ideas, spend some time getting deeply acquainted with the place where your trees will be growing. Your aim is to gather as much information as possible so that when you sit down to select trees and plants, you will have a deep understanding of the climate and the site in which they will grow. This will go a long way in helping you match the right plant with the right place.

When you're working with a small orchard space, having a map or plan of your site on which to record your observations and base your design can be very helpful. You might already have an acceptable site plan, or you could hire a surveyor or landscape architect to create one for you. That might make sense for you, especially if you have other projects that call for more precise plans. Or use Google Maps or a similar Internet map site to find and print an image of you property and work from that—depending on tree cover and resolution, this might or might not be helpful. If the image offers a good view, print the image, take it to a copy shop, and enlarge it to a useful size. Then lay tracing paper over the image and start writing down observations and exploring different ideas.

Get to know the broad climatic patterns, or macroclimate, of the region and progress toward an intimate understanding of the specifics, or microclimate, of your property.

This is not the first dusting of snow this mature peach tree has seen.

HARDINESS ZONE AVERAGE ANNUAL LOWEST TEMPERATURES

HARDINESS ZONE	TEMPERATURE (°F)	TEMPERATURE (°C)
1	Below –50	Below –46
2	–50 to –40	–46 to –40
3	–40 to –30	–40 to –34
4	–30 to –20	–34 to –29
5	–20 to –10	–29 to –23
6	–10 to 0	–23 to –18
7	0 to 10	–18 to –12
8	10 to 20	–12 to –7
9	20 to 30	–7 to –1
10	30 to 40	–1 to 4

MACROCLIMATE

Lots of great resources are available to help you learn about the broad climatic patterns at play where you live. Many areas of the United States are served by a cooperative extension service, and thriving Master Gardener communities exist throughout the United States and Canada. These organizations can be a wellspring of local knowledge, and even in this modern age, they can often provide better information than what you'll find on the Internet. A local nursery is another great place to get information about climate and the types of trees that are best suited to your area.

You can learn a lot about a particular plant by looking at the hardiness zone rating on the nursery tag. This rating refers to an area's average lowest annual temperature and provides an indication of whether a plant will survive the winter in that area. Some gardeners see a plant hardiness rating as a challenge, and some green thumbs are tempted to plant a banana in Chicago. I must admit to enjoying a bit of that myself, but I am just as proud of my perfectly ripe 'Gravenstein' apple (a local treasure) as I am of the greenhouse papayas I've plucked.

If you are new to fruit growing, I suggest you get a few harvests under your belt, with the types of fruit you see offered at your local farmers' market. Before long, you'll be bragging to your relatives in some cushy climate about your nearly year-round bounty.

Another important parameter you will want to know is the average number of *chill hours* for your area. Although this probably brings to mind an afternoon spent enjoying a couple of beers in your backyard, this term is used in the gardening world to quantify the number of hours that your dormant trees will spend "chilling" below 45°F. It is an important statistic, because specific fruit tree varieties require different chill hours to set fruit. Apples, peaches, nectarines, cherries, and apricots are the most sensitive to chill hours, and if you are gardening in a low-chill area, be sure to check the chilling needs of each variety you will be planting. Keep in mind that local knowledge of what has historically performed well in your area is better than anything you read in a book. The specific observations that you make about your yard and chats with the old-timers in your neighborhood will give you a better sense of what you can plant.

ADDiTiONAL ZONE iNFORMATiON

Learn more information about hardiness zones through the U.S. Department of Agriculture's U.S. National Arboretum site at www.usna.usda.gov/Hardzone/ushzmap.html or via the Sunset climate zone maps at www.sunset.com/garden/climate-zones, which consider a much wider range of climatic factors, such as latitude, elevation, and ocean influence. The Sunset resource has been expanded to encompass the whole of the United States and parts of Canada. Hopefully, this classification will continue to be developed, because it is a great resource for the fruit grower.

MICROCLIMATE

Lay tracing paper over an image or scale plan of your yard and use it to record layers of specific information about the microclimate at your site. I like to note information about several key factors.

SUN Which areas get the most sun? Assign a grade to different areas: A for more than 8 hours of sun, B for better than 6 hours, C for 4½ hours, and so on. Afternoon sun is more intense than morning sun, so if one area receives 4 hours of morning sun and another gets 4 hours of afternoon sun, plant the more heat-loving trees on the afternoon side.

TOPOGRAPHY Take advantage of variations in topography. In mild climates, for example, plant citrus (which does not tolerate frost) higher up on a slope and apples (which tend to require more chill hours) lower down the slope where cold air settles.

SOIL TYPES Is the soil better in some areas and worse in others? Look for wet areas and improve the drainage (with drains or by regrading the site) prior to planting. You might need to import soil to improve drainage or soil structure in a particular area.

WIND From which direction does the wind blow, and could it be easily buffered? A vine-covered trellis that lets some air circulate through makes a better wind buffer than a solid wall.

VIEWS Sightlines in and out of your yard might need to be enhanced or screened.

SEASONALITY Think about how each of the elements on this list is important in each season. It is easy to forget about a drainage problem in the dry season or to forget how much shade that bigleaf maple will cast next summer.

THINGS TO COME Think about the future. Does a neighbor plan to build up a second story that might shade parts of your property, or is the city going to replace water lines next year and dig up part of your yard.

Beginning the Design

As you survey your yard, picture all the ways that this space will reflect who you are. You know it will reflect your palate, because you're going to plant the fruits (and possibly herbs and vegetables) that you like to eat. Are you a swimmer or water-lover who likes the sounds of a small fountain tucked into a corner? Do you need a space to meditate or a sandbox for your growing brood? Sure, you want to plant some trees, but this is also a good time to consider where to place a bistro table to enjoy your morning tea and paper.

I like to start most design projects by making a bunch of lists. I start with conceptual lists that include words that

Spring rain showers blowing in from the west

will describe my finished garden and move toward the more pragmatic. The great thing about a list is that it can be easily prioritized, which always seems to be necessary. At the start, I like to channel some of the kids I've worked with to create school gardens. If you ask a kid to make a list of things she wants in a garden, she'll come up with a lot of impractical, but nonetheless fun and exciting suggestions (a waterslide, a trampoline, a petting zoo). My guess is that if you allow your imagination to run wild, you'll come up with some out-of-the-box ideas that have the potential to make you garden one-of-a-kind. It's also totally acceptable to refer to that file of pictures from designs you like and flag certain elements that you want to incorporate here.

Lots of elements can be included in a small yard along with fruit trees.

Arbor	Fire pit	Rock garden
Barbecue area	Fountain	Sauna
Bench	Gazebo	Shed
Berry patch	Hammock	Sink
Chickens	Hot tub	Sleeping porch
Compost pile	Lawn	Vegetables
Cottage	Paths	Vineyard
Deck or patio	Play structure	Woodpile
Dining area	Pool	
Espalier	Pond	

The design process tends to be cyclical, so as you play with your ideas, remember to go outside often, look around town to see what your neighbors are doing in their gardens, and stay open to new ideas. If this is your first garden design undertaking, solicit help from friends or professionals and have fun with it. It might seem tedious to invest all this effort before you've planted even a single tree, but the money you save in headache medicine will more than justify it.

Let's look at a few of these in more detail, with our fruit trees in mind.

CHICKENS

A small flock of chickens is a great addition to a garden. Four birds, a small coop, and a narrow run equal happiness: chickens contribute to the productivity and health of your backyard. They love to peck at fallen fruit and can help control insect pests. And after you've eaten a fresh egg provided by one of your birds, you'll have a hard time going out for breakfast.

Chickens like the same environment enjoyed by fruit trees (sunny, well-drained, and so on), and they love to roost in low branches. They will also eat from your vegetable garden, so when designing your garden, consider adding a chicken run or reserve another space just for them. Lightweight, moveable fencing can be used to create flexible chicken yards that are easy to manage. You can let the birds fun free, but remember that although their manure does fertilize your garden, it will stick to your shoes.

COMPOST PILE

If you have the room to spare, an area for making compost can serve as the digestive system for your edible landscape. It doesn't have to be a stinky pile of rotting scraps either. Regular turning and moisture monitoring will help your piles stay active and aerobic, a key to making good compost. Rather than hide your heap, build a simple trellis structure overhead and plant it with a fragrant climbing rose.

In smaller spaces, worms can do an amazing job of converting a relatively small amount of kitchen scraps that a family creates into the highest quality plant food. An actively managed three-bin compost system could take up around 100 square feet, but a single worm bin, another great way to create organic fertilizer out of meat-free table scraps, can be kept under your sink.

DECK OR PATIO

Fruit trees can be integrated into the design of your deck or patio. Trees planted directly in the soil tend to perform better over time, so consider incorporating planting wells into your patio design. Planter boxes can be designed to extend all the way down to terra firma and can incorporate an open bottom for drainage and root penetration. These spaces can often create warm microclimates—even leaving a stone out of a flagstone patio provides space to add a citrus tree or other heat lover that might not thrive in other parts of your yard. Potted trees can also help the space feel less bare and more a part of your larger landscape.

ESPALIER

This centuries-old technique is a beautiful way to utilize the many linear spaces that are created around an urban or suburban home. Driveways and fence lines that get enough sun are no-brainers for espalier. A sun-facing chimney can be the ideal spot to train a less hardy variety that would appreciate the reflected heat from that thermal mass. Replace those old pickets with a cable fence designed just for your trees. I like to use 4-by-4 or larger posts for an espalier fence and add copper end caps or other details to make them year-round features in the landscape. Three or four horizontal cables spaced 18 inches apart can create a clean, simple espalier, but don't be afraid to get creative with the forms.

LAWN

Sod and fruit trees are not the best bedfellows, because they compete in the same soil zone for water and nutrients. Lawns also need frequent short irrigation cycles, while fruit trees do better with less frequent, longer waterings. Focus tree-watering efforts starting at a point about halfway between the trunk and out toward the drip line (the area just below the outermost leaves). The more efficient water uptake roots are near a tree's drip line. Closer to the trunk, the roots tend to be crowded and compete for the same resources in the soil. Too much water at the base of the tree can decrease the amount of air in the soil, resulting in fungal disease and soil pests. (Try to keep sod, and the water it needs, outside your tree's drip line.)

PATHS

Paths can do a lot to create a welcoming feeling in your garden, especially in the dormant season when not much is going on out there. Around fruit trees, a soft, permeable pathway of

Chickens eat insect pests, make and spread fertilizer, and give you yummy eggs.

This good-looking organic matter is on its way to becoming great compost.

Make a beautiful old stone garden wall even better by adding a well-trained fan espalier.

Chef Mike Emanuel's magical cob oven

mulch or woodchips will allow the roots better access to water and air and even provide a gentle landing place for fallen fruit. Decomposed granite, also called gold path fines, is another attractive path material, but beware: the tiny stones are easily tracked indoors and can scratch hardwood flooring.

SHED

As you are starting to realize, lots of tools and other stuff can come in handy as you care for an edible landscape. In my experience, that care is more likely to get done if the tools you need are close at hand. A beautiful shed, perhaps one that matches the architecture of your home, is the perfect place to store this stuff; it can be a nice focal point in your yard or part of another structure such as a sleeping porch or woodshed. Add a pegboard for hanging pruning equipment and some hooks for hand tools to help reduce clutter.

VEGETABLES

Fruit and vegetables go together like peaches and peas. My guess is that you already have (or are considering adding) a space to grow seasonal produce in addition to fruit trees. The obvious consideration when integrating the two is shade. A well-placed fruit tree can provide a welcome shelter from afternoon sun for lettuces or other cool-season veggies and can help them produce longer into the season. I have had very good success growing vegetables year-round between the rows of a young orchard. Espalier is a natural choice for bordering a vegetable plot, and espaliered trees can make the space look beautiful as well as productive.

VINEYARD OR BERRY PATCH

Grapes, cane berries, and even currants perform well on a trellis structure similar to that used for espaliered trees, and the two can be combined to good effect. Layering your planting is also a good option with berries, as they grow as an understory plant in the wild. I like the idea of a four- or five-layer espalier fence with berries, grapes, and/or currants growing below a taller apple or pear structure. Round out your fruit planting with these adaptable and hardy plants

WOOD-FIRED COB OVEN

It is interesting to realize that all the ovens I'm thinking about are surrounded by fruit trees. Some of the tastiest fruit dishes I've eaten have been baked in cob ovens. If you like to cook, consider setting aside a prominent place in your yard, not too far from your kitchen, and building a wood-fired oven.

Several friends and I have used an excellent book, *Build Your Own Earth Oven*, by Kiko Denzer, as a guide to do just that, and it has changed the way we gather for meals. Building with earth is an ancient technique that has been used by countless cultures to build everything from full-sized homes to tiny wood-fired ovens. The term *cob* generally refers to a mixture of sand and clay that can also include straw, hair, and dung. For small projects, the mixture can be combined by foot, applying water and adjusting the ratios to create the perfect texture. The cob mixture is then formed into the desired shape, in this case over a dome of sand used to support the oven's form.

Tossing small bundles of fruit tree prunings into the fire can add great flavor to grilled meats and other dishes. Take care to select wood that has not been sprayed recently and tie it up with twine to dry. Toss a few sticks on the fire toward the end of cooking to get the most fruit flavor.

Design Ideas

Three case studies will hopefully help get some ideas flowing as you design your space. With a little planning, you can create a garden of your own that is both edible and ornamental.

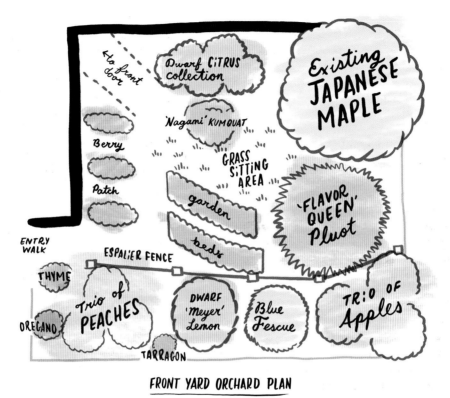

FRONT YARD ORCHARD PLAN

FRONT YARD DESIGN

My friends Terence and Stephanie had never been happy with the landscape in their front yard. After a neighbor removed some large redwoods that were shading the space, this newfound sun exposure had them itching to plant more edibles. In addition to a couple of veggie beds, fruit trees, and herbs, they wanted a place to sit out front and enjoy a Sunday morning cup of coffee. There is a great sense of community on this block and the neighborhood kids all play in the street. Stephanie liked the idea of having a space that was somewhat private, but she also wanted to work or relax in her garden while her kids bustled around the 'hood.

Three tree forms are represented in this design: the espalier fence, dwarf citrus, and open-center pluot. The meandering espalier fence is set back from the sidewalk, so that part of the yard is shared with the neighborhood. Garden beds and a sitting area behind the espalier create a more personal space that is also more secure for small children. Low-growing culinary herbs along the entry walkway allow easy access to that sprig of thyme needed in a recipe. A berry patch, dwarf citrus, and a pluot fill out the perimeter of this edible front yard oasis.

Terence and Stephanie love to cook with citrus, so a collection of dwarf citrus was selected as a foundation planting. The trio, or 3-in-1 plantings, consist of early-season, midseason, and late-season varieties for extended harvest. Low-growing ornamental grasses are reminiscent of orchards past. In this front yard, there's not a day without at least something to anticipate harvesting.

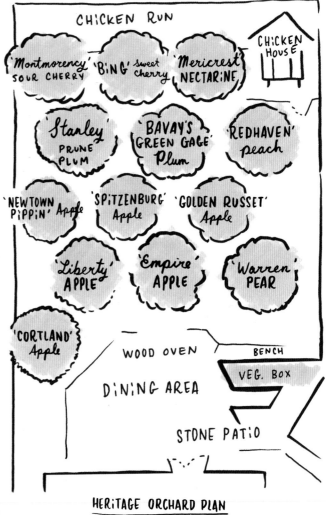

HERITAGE ORCHARD PLAN

HERITAGE ORCHARD

A young and successful chef recently bought a house in an upstate New York neighborhood with a severely neglected backyard. He was inspired to create a small orchard that recalled the historic agriculture of the state. Wood-fired cooking is his specialty, so a clay oven was essential. He also wanted to be able to provide herbs, eggs, and a few veggies for his restaurant, and he wanted to include an area to get together with staff and friends.

A minor tweak on the traditional orchard grid, in this design, semi-dwarf trees are laid out in offset rows, allowing for tighter 12-foot spacing. The oven is the focal point, and the chef envisions this outdoor hearth becoming a community hangout, similar to the village bread ovens of earlier generations. A chicken run along the back fence gives the birds a place to roam while keeping them out of the vegetable garden. Raised boxes are filled with herbs and vegetables for home and restaurant use.

New York isn't called The Big Apple for nuthin'. A primary goal for this orchard design was to include apple varieties that either had regional significance or were heirlooms with an interesting story or special use. Other fruit trees in the mix include pear, peach, nectarine, sweet and sour cherries, and plum.

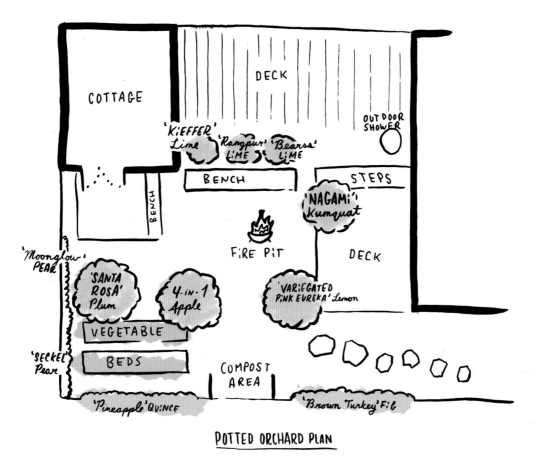

POTTED ORCHARD PLAN

CONTAINER ORCHARD

Erin Kunkel, whose photography you have been enjoying in this book, lives in the Sunset neighborhood of San Francisco. Whenever the fog allows, Erin and her husband, Danny Hess, a well-known maker of custom wooden surfboards, like to sit by the campfire with friends after a day in the water. And what better way to refuel after a surf session than with some tasty home-grown fruit? Okay, after a beer.

The soil in Erin's yard is difficult to distinguish from beach sand, so, for this design, we are planting primarily in pots. The marine influence is unmistakable in the climate and ambiance of this yard. Wind and fog are nearly constant reminders that the great Pacific Ocean is a short skateboard ride away. Fencing helps to dampen the wind and has actually created a pretty warm microclimate. Selected plants don't require too much in the way of heat or chill, but a couple of plants in this design push the envelope a bit.

**Erin and Danny's yard
during planting**

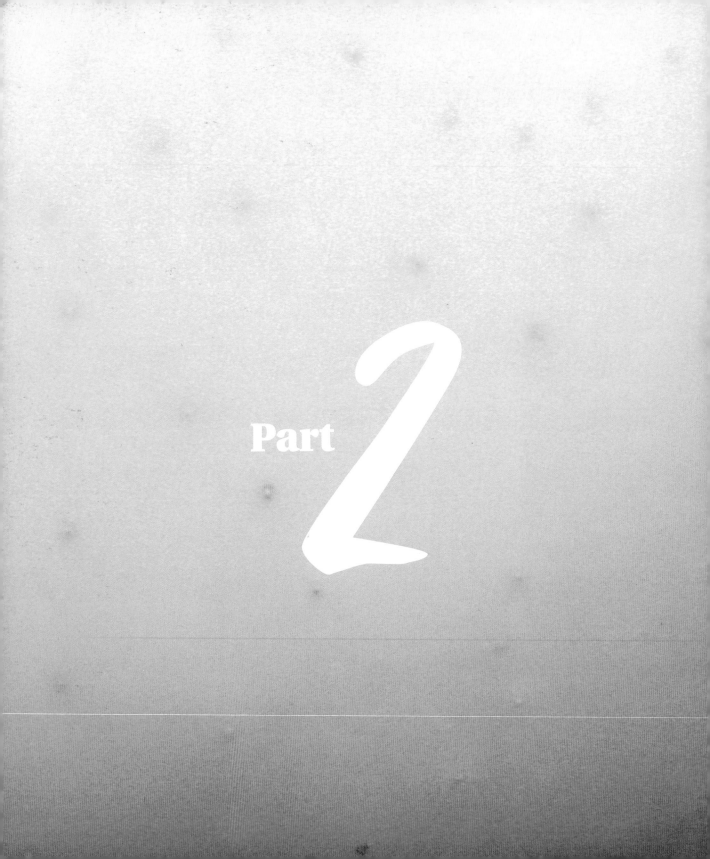

Part 2

Fruit Tree Guide:
The Family Album

Choosing Plants for Your Orchard

By now you are getting into the design process and hopefully starting to get comfortable with how it toggles your mind back and forth between the general and the specific. If you have been working over one scheme for a while and it still isn't feeling right, try making a fundamental change to the design concept. If you've used a lot of straight lines, try to add some more organic shapes to the mix.

Peaches in flower in spring

Identify the dominant feature in the landscape and play with removing it completely and redesigning without it. After you settle on a general design concept that you like, tally up the number of spaces you have for fruit trees and get ready to make some hard choices.

Choosing fruit trees and plants for your backyard orchard is always an exciting task, but with the huge range of trees available, it can be tough to decide what will work best for you. It is amazing (and maybe a little overwhelming) to look over the number of varieties that are available. Each year a few new varieties come to my attention that send me out into my yard thinking there's got to be a spot I can squeeze in another tree or two. And there usually is.

Most places that have been settled for more than a few decades have at least one specific variety of fruit associated with them. I grew up in 'Gravenstein' apple country and now live in 'Imperial Epineuse' plum land, although 'Cabernet Sauvignon' grapes have lately become the new emblem. Discovering the fruit mascot for a given borough can give you a wonderful insight into the climate of a region as well as a sense of connection to the history and people of that place.

Finally, as mouthwatering as it might be, reading variety descriptions in a book is no substitute for actually tasting some fruit. Your local farmers' market or produce stand in season is a great place to familiarize yourself with varieties that will likely do well in your area. You are sure to find more diversity here than at the grocery store, and most stands offer samples so you can taste before you buy. Fruit growers tend to be pretty nice folks and are generally happy to share their experience with certain varieties, and you might just make a valued friend in the process. Some nurseries also host fruit tastings in summer and fall that, for a fruit lover like you, are worth the time spent away from afternoon chores.

The Two-Part Tree

A majority of the fruit varieties discussed in these pages will be offered to you for sale as grafted stock, consisting of a rootstock and a scion (the variety). Look near the base of most fruit trees and you will find a distinctive jog in its form. This is the graft union. We use grafting and asexual propagation (plant cloning) to come up with a tree that is true to its name, or true to type. Trees produced from seeds are often not true to type. As Michael Pollan pointed out in his book *Botany of Desire*, the seeds that folk hero Johnny Appleseed was sowing did not come true to type and were used mainly for making hard cider. It can be a little mind boggling to think that from a single 'Fuji' apple tree, for example, we have clipped little twigs and buds, grafted them onto new roots, and today every 'Fuji' tree ever planted is a clone of the original tree.

You'll find quite a large selection when it comes to the foundation of a tree: the rootstock. After you have an idea of the type of fruit you want to grow, try to find a rootstock that suits your site. A good rootstock—one of the top five most important factors for a successful tree planting—is:

A hardy variety,

that fits the chill hours for the area,

that is resistant to local diseases,

that is grafted on a rootstock that is suited to your soil (and disease pressure, and other local factors), and

that is planted in a sunny and well-drained spot.

CHOOSING A ROOTSTOCK TO FIT YOUR SPACE

Your first thought when you're selecting a rootstock is the size of tree you want. This is an okay place to start, but keep in mind that the ultimate size and shape of your trees is in your hands (no, not this book). Without summer pruning or other techniques to reduce vigor, semi-dwarf can easily mean a tree that is 15 feet tall or taller.

My hand is holding the rootstock, and everything above my hand is the scion; notice the graft union just above my hand.

GRAFTED VERSUS GENETIC DWARF TREES

Grafted dwarf trees are created by grafting a regular-size variety on a dwarfing rootstock to produce a more compact tree. Genetic dwarf trees are created by propagating a naturally compact variety on a standard-size rootstock. Genetic dwarf trees usually have closely spaced leaves and growth buds.

When shopping for trees, look for a second, usually lower, tag on the trunk to learn about the rootstock.

In most cases, you will be deciding between dwarf and semi-dwarf trees. As a general rule, I prefer semi-dwarf, because they tend to be stronger trees that require less staking and training. (An exception might be the newer dwarf cherries, which I have found to be quite productive and robust for a dwarf tree; plus they're easy to net for bird protection.)

Some trees are natural or genetic dwarfs. But most dwarf and semi-dwarf trees you'll find in nurseries are standard trees that have been grafted onto a size-controlling rootstock. Semi-dwarf rootstocks generally produce a tree that is about half the size of the standard tree's height—great if your fruit tree would generally top out at about 25 feet, not so great if it would generally reach 40 feet or more. Dwarf rootstocks do produce smaller trees, generally about 25 to 30 percent smaller than a standard tree, and usually in the 6 to 10 foot range. These are just general ranges, however; some fruit trees grafted on a semi-dwarf rootstock can be 80 percent of the standard tree size, and some dwarf trees can reach close to 50 percent.

Your best bet is to look on the nursery tag or ask nursery experts exactly what the rootstock is for any tree you're considering. Some common rootstocks and the general size the tree will reach are listed in the accompanying table, although new rootstocks are being developed every year. These are general guidelines and are not a guarantee of final tree size, as factors such as climate and siting as well as individual plant vigor also play a role. Even with a dwarf rootstock, you might still need to include summer pruning to keep the tree in bounds in a small orchard.

COMMON ROOTSTOCKS

TREE	ROOTSTOCK NAME	SIZE
Apple	Bud 9	4–10 ft.
	G.11	12–16 ft.
	G.16	9–14 ft.
	G.30	12–15 ft.
	EMLA 26	8–14 ft.
	EMLA 27	4–10 ft.
	M.7	12–14 ft.
	M.9	6–10 ft.
	M.26	8–12 ft.
	M.27	4–8 ft.
	MM.106	12–14 ft.
	MM.111	15–20 ft.
	'Mark' (MAC 9)	8–12 ft.
	P.22	4–8 ft.
Apricot	'Citation'	12–18 ft.
	'St. Julien A'	10–12 ft.
	'Torinel'	10–12 ft.
Cherry	3CRI78	6–8 ft.
	'Colt'	12–15 ft.
	'Gisela 5'	8–10 ft.
	'Gisela 6'	8–14 ft.
	'Krymsk 5'	10 ft.
Citrus	'Flying Dragon'	5–7 ft.
Peach and nectarine	'Citation'	8–14 ft.
	'Pixy'	8–10 ft.
	'St. Julien A'	10–12 ft.
Pear and quince	OHx333	12–18 ft.
	Quince A	10–20 ft.
	Quince C	8–18 ft.
Plum hybrids	'Citation'	12–18 ft.
	'Pixy'	8–10 ft.
	'St. Julien A'	10–12 ft.

The Family Album

The Family Album explores the most common and some uncommon fruit trees that might be right for your space. To make it easier to understand what trees might work well in your yard and also coexist easily, fruit trees are grouped by their families. Just as human families share similar characteristics, so do fruit trees in the same plant family. They often have the same growing requirements and climate preferences. On the other hand, they can also share some of the same susceptibility to pests and diseases.

The largest family, in terms of numbers of different fruits, is the stone fruit family, which encompasses some of the most familiar fruits, including peaches, plums, and cherries. Not quite as large in terms of the number of family members, but equally large if not larger in the number of varieties, are the members of the pome family—namely apples, pears, and quince. Members of the citrus family don't thrive in nearly as many climate zones as the stone and pome fruits, but a surprisingly large number of trees are available, each with its own special characteristics, for those lucky enough to live in an area where citrus grow.

You'll find descriptions of each tree and fruit, general planting and care instructions, pruning and harvest advice, and some of the best varieties. It's up to you to decide which is best for your mini-orchard.

Dwarf citrus provides a bright accent to the winter landscape.

Stone FRUITS

These are the fruits of summer. They're the tart cherries, the sweet and delicate apricots, the lushly juicy peaches and nectarines, the versatile plums. They get their name from the single stone, or pit, held at the center of the fruit rather than seeds.

All stone fruits are of the genus *Prunus*. In addition to their characteristic center stone, they are all thought to have originated in

With its graceful form and sweet fruit, a semi-dwarf 'Blenheim' apricot is the perfect addition to this side yard garden plot.

Europe. Since then, the trees have spread across a good portion of the world and have developed their own distinctive cultural needs.

If your climate is amenable, you can grow all of these fruits with little trouble. Good growing locales, however, aren't so widespread. Stone fruits tend to have fewer problems in the relatively milder climates of western North America. They don't do as well in either very harsh or very warm climates, and humid conditions can also be a problem, although peaches in particular thrive in the humid summers of the southeastern United States. But even if you can't grow every one of them, some stone fruits can be grown in marginal areas if you're willing to search out the appropriate varieties and take some extra care with protection and pest and disease control. So if you garden in northern Minnesota, you might not be able to grow apricots or sweet cherries, but sour cherries and hardy plum hybrids are still possibilities there.

Another advantage for home gardeners is that many smaller varieties of stone fruits are being developed. In addition, most stone fruit trees take well to summer pruning, which keeps their size manageable and the fruit readily accessible. Other options for growing the most fruit in a small space include grafting several varieties onto one rootstock and planting more than one dwarf tree in a single hole.

Even if you can't grow some of the varieties included here, you might be able to try them out if you can find them in markets or on your travels. They're all worth a taste.

A bounty of peaches at the farmers' market

Many folks prefer the smooth skin of the nectarine. Yum.

Peaches and Nectarines

After you've tasted a tree-ripened peach, you'll find it difficult, if not impossible, to eat the rock-solid peaches you find in most grocery stores. A tree-ripened peach is so juicy you need to bend over while you eat it so the juices will drip off your hands and onto the ground rather than onto your clothing. The taste of a store-bought peach, even one that is left to ripen on the countertop, pales in comparison to that of a fresh peach.

Nectarines are often said to be a cross between a peach and a plum, but they are in fact a type of peach (*Prunus persica* var. *nucipersica*), most likely a mutation that developed naturally. Not that you can't tell a nectarine from a standard peach even at a quick glance. It's not just the lack of fuzz; nectarines tend to be a deeper red or yellow color. Most are slightly smaller than a peach, and nectarine lovers insist that they are sweeter. If you can grow peaches, you can grow nectarines, and many home gardeners grow both.

The flavor of a tree-picked peach or nectarine is reason enough to add a tree to your small orchard. An added bonus is the ornamental nature of the trees themselves. They have a naturally open and spreading shape, and in spring, they are covered with pink blossoms. Their long, drooping summer leaves provide a bright, deep-green focal point in your garden. Come fall, the leaves turn from yellow to a brilliant orange before dropping.

CHOOSING A PEACH OR NECTARINE: THE BASICS

There is a peach variety for practically every gardener; narrowing it down is the problem. Fewer nectarine varieties are available, but you have many good ones from which to choose. Your first step should be to check with nurseries and your local cooperative extension service or other agricultural agency to find out which varieties grow where you live. Then decide whether you want a clingstone, a freestone, or a semi-freestone fruit; a white or yellow peach or nectarine; a tree that produces fruit early, midseason, or late; and a standard or dwarf tree.

My buddy Francisco enjoys a tree-ripened nectarine.

This sounds like a lot of decisions, but it's fairly straightforward. Cling peaches and nectarines are the best choice for canning; freestone and semi-freestone fruits are generally considered the best for eating fresh and baking. Within both categories, you'll find fruits with white or yellow flesh. Those with white flesh tend to be slightly sweeter, and yellow-fleshed fruit is generally slightly more acidic, but there are no hard and fast rules. What matters most is the flavor you like the best.

Fruit appearance and ripening times also vary. The classic peach shape is round, with yellow-red, fuzzy skin. These days, though, you'll find peaches that are flatter and in colors that range from almost yellow when fully ripe to a deep, deep red. And although midsummer is usually considered prime peach season, some peach varieties ripen earlier and others are not ready until early autumn. Nectarine skin color also ranges from white to deep red, and the ripening season is equally long. With some judicious choices, you can easily extend your fruit growing season to last throughout the summer.

A standard peach or nectarine tree can easily reach up to 25 feet tall and just as wide, but most can be trained to around 10 feet tall for ease in picking the fruit. For small gardens, though, even a 10-foot-tall tree can seem overpowering. Fortunately, a number of dwarf varieties are available, some of which can even be grown in large containers. These trees also can handle being espaliered, grafted with more than one variety on a single trunk, or planted with several varieties in a single hole. Almost all are self-fertile, so you needn't worry about having to plant several varieties to get fruit.

GROWING PEACHES AND NECTARINES

Peach and nectarine trees are more demanding than most fruit trees when it comes to where they grow and the care they need. Choosing a variety that will thrive in your climate is essential, of course, as is finding the appropriate growing conditions within your space. In addition, they require year-round care, from pruning in winter and fertilizing and watering throughout the growing season, to rigorous thinning and dealing with fungal diseases and other problems.

Overall, peaches and nectarines do best in areas with some winter chill but no extended periods of heavy freezing or late frosts. They also prefer hot and dry, or dryish, summers—for example, they grow well in California, parts of British Columbia, and most of the southeastern United States. Maritime climates generally lack the summer heat these fruits need, but an early-ripening variety planted against a sunny wall is certainly worth a try.

GETTING STARTED Most trees are sold as bare-root plants, although you might find some in containers. Bare-root peaches and nectarines should be planted in late winter or early spring, as soon as the ground can be worked and frosts are no longer expected. Container-grown trees can be planted from autumn through spring and even into summer, although you should avoid planting if the weather is too hot. Look for a spot with full sun exposure and well-drained soil; add amendments before planting if your soil is either heavy clay or overly sandy.

GROWING SEASON CARE Like most fruits and vegetables, peaches and nectarines require regular watering, especially throughout the spring and summer. Set a watering schedule, and be sure to water deeply. To help conserve water and inhibit weed growth, spread mulch around the tree, but keep it about 3 inches away from the trunk. Keep the ground and mulch relatively soft and smooth so that it's easy to pick up branch thinnings and so that fruit that falls from the tree avoids being badly bruised.

These trees are heavy feeders. Get them off to a good start by fertilizing with a complete, balanced (up to 10-10-10) fertilizer about a week after planting. Then fertilize heavily, again with a complete fertilizer, each year in early spring. You might need to adapt the regimen to add more nitrogen (the first number of the three) if the tree shows signs of depleted iron (leaves turn yellow starting at the edges, and the veins remain green—this could also indicate too much water, so check that first).

After the trees start bearing fruit, thinning is essential. Difficult as it might be to remove potential fruit, you'll end up with larger and juicier fruit if you're ruthless about this. Thinning is also better for younger trees, because it keeps them from being overburdened and becoming misshapen by too much fruit clinging to a single branch.

Peaches and nectarines will drop some fruit, usually in early summer, but you'll have to supplement this natural thinning. The general rule used to be to leave a fist-width of space between each fruit; now the recommendation is to leave about 8 inches. If two or three fruits are growing too close together, prune to leave only one in place. Also, remove developing fruit forming on the ends of small branches so the branches won't break under the weight. Be prepared to go over the tree several times; your eye will see new fruits that you'll swear weren't there before.

HARVESTING Depending on the variety, peaches and nectarines can be ready to pick any time from early summer to early autumn. The fruit should have a full color with no green showing and be slightly soft to the touch when very gently squeezed (use your palm to avoid bruising). Fully ripened fruit can be easily twisted off the tree at the stem. This can be a balancing act; ideally, pick fruit that is fully ripe before it falls off the tree or is eaten by birds or squirrels. But even if you miss your window of opportunity, slightly damaged fruit can be salvaged. Simply cut off the bad spots and eat it fresh or use it for cooking. Once the harvest starts, be prepared for an onslaught of fruit—it's a short but intense season.

Tip pruning a peach at the pink bud stage, which is also a great time to spray the tree for leaf curl

PRUNING

All peaches and nectarines, even dwarf varieties, need to be pruned regularly and heavily, although genetic dwarf varieties won't require quite as much pruning as standard trees. Most fruit develops on one- and two-year–old branches, so pruning encourages more branching and more fruit. You should also remove diseased and dead branches and keep the shape of the tree open enough to encourage fruit development throughout the tree and not just on the outer branches. In the case of standard trees, pruning keeps the trees to a manageable size, usually 10 to 12 feet. Prune when the tree is dormant or, in colder climates, in early spring.

The pruning process should start as soon as you plant the tree. Cut the main stem, or trunk, at a slight angle and above a bud, or ideally (for an open-center tree) above a series of three to five buds spaced evenly around the stem both horizontally and vertically. After the first year, select three branches and begin to shape the tree; an open vase shape is best.

For mature trees, cut back two-thirds of the previous year's growth or cut back each branch by about two-thirds. For dwarf selections, prune to keep the tree to the desired size and to keep it open. For all trees, remove dead, diseased or damaged, and crossing branches.

Don't feel obligated to keep your peach or nectarine as a standard tree form. They can also be espaliered against a wall, which is an ideal spot for helping trees stay warmer in cold climates. If you're growing in a very small area, summer pruning will help keep the tree size in check.

PESTS AND DISEASES

Peach leaf curl and brown rot are the most likely diseases you'll encounter with a peach tree. Peach leaf curl is probably the most easily recognized: leaves curl up and look puckered and discolored. It is a common problem, but wet climates will exacerbate it. In trees with brown rot, the twigs crack and sap oozes out while flowers wilt. A third disease, peach scab, is more of a problem in the southern United States. The fruit is covered with small green or black spots. After these diseases have taken hold, you will need to wait until autumn to control them. Other potential problems include the peach tree borer and marauding squirrels and birds.

The first step for disease and pest prevention is simply good garden care. Growing conditions should be optimal; trees weakened by stress will be more susceptible to problems. Keep the area around the tree free of leaves, fallen fruit, weeds, and other debris. Keep garden tools clean as well. Remove diseased branches as soon as possible, and do not dispose of them in your compost pile.

If a tree develops peach leaf curl, brown rot, or peach scab, wait until it is bare in the fall and then spray with a dormant spray of either lime sulfur or fixed copper. Follow up with another dose in late winter or early spring when the buds have appeared and are starting to swell but haven't yet opened. After the tree flowers, spraying will have no effect.

Peach tree borers tend to attack trees that are already weak. You'll recognize an infestation by the brownish jelly substance weeping from holes in the trunk at the base of the tree. Peach tree borers can easily kill a young tree. If you see insect damage near the base of a tree, use a small screwdriver or similar tool to dig out the borer. Check with local authorities at your nursery or cooperative extension for the best methods for controlling these pests as soon as you notice symptoms.

Animals are trickier to manage. Realistically, you'll probably have to resign yourself to some fruit loss. Try netting the tree about two or three weeks before the fruit is ripe, or hang shiny objects in trees to scare away birds. Some people swear by fake predators, such as owls, but move them periodically so the birds won't start to ignore them.

Gummosis is a general term for this type of oozing sap. Keeping the orchard clean can be a big help, which would include removing that mummified peach from last season.

A sticky barrier of plant resin can be great prevention against aphids, scale, and earwigs (with can cause scarring on the fruit skin), but it won't keep away peach tree borers.

Peaches

PEACH & NECTARINE VARIETIES

Literally hundreds of peach trees and a fairly large number of nectarine varieties are available. Included here are some of the most popular varieties for home gardens. Check with local nurseries and cooperative extension agents for recommendations for your area.

ARCTIC SUPREME

Sweet white clingstone that ripens in midseason. Great flavor.

EARLIGRANDE

Early peach with yellow flesh. Semi-freestone with great flavor. Good low-chill variety for warmer climates.

FROST

Yellow freestone that ripens midseason to late; resistant to peach leaf curl.

GLEASON EARLY ELBERTA

(*or* 'Lemon Elberta', 'Improved Elberta')
Hardy freestone with yellow flesh. Great flavor. Try 'Elberta' and other offshoots of this popular tree.

INDIAN BLOOD CLING

(*or* 'Indian Cling')
Old variety that ripens late. Flesh is yellow and red and very sweet. Good for end-of-summer peach cravings.

INDIAN FREE

Classic heirloom freestone peach with green-white skin, yellow flesh, and a somewhat tart taste that ripens mid- to late-season. Resistant to peach leaf curl. One of the few peaches that needs pollinating.

LORING

Early-ripening freestone with large yellow fruit, good flavor, and less fuzz than most.

NECTAR

Great tasting white freestone that ripens in early midseason.

REDHAVEN

Popular yellow, semi-freestone peach that ripens early and continues ripening longer than most peaches. Great for canning or freezing.

Peaches <small>continued</small>

Dwarf

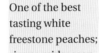

REDSKIN

Midseason freestone with yellow flesh that is a good all-around peach for eating fresh or for canning or freezing.

RELIANCE

Early-ripening yellow freestone that is cold hardy.

SNOW BEAUTY

One of the best tasting white freestone peaches; ripens midseason.

STRAWBERRY FREE

Favorite white-fleshed freestone ripens in early midseason.

TROPIC SNOW

Early white-fleshed freestone with wonderful flavor; needs less chilling than most white peaches.

BONANZA II

Genetic dwarf, midseason ripener with deep yellow flesh and a stronger peach flavor than 'Bonanza', another dwarf variety.

Peaches

Nectarines

EL DORADO

Genetic dwarf with early yellow-fleshed fruit. Freestone variety with good flavor.

PIX ZEE

Genetic dwarf ripens in the early part of the midseason. Yellow flesh is nicely flavored.

ARCTIC ROSE

Wonderfully sweet semi-freestone with white flesh and whitish skin tinged with red. Ripens midseason. Others in the 'Arctic' series include 'Arctic Fantasy' (improved version of 'Fantasia'), '

Arctic Glo' (an early ripener), 'Arctic Jay' (large, ripens relatively early), and 'Arctic Sun' (early semi-freestone, with red skin; good for low-chill areas).

FANTASIA

Large freestone nectarine with yellow flesh, red and white skin, and sweet taste. Ripens midseason; doesn't require as much chilling as other nectarine varieties but still good in colder regions.

GOLDMINE

Popular choice for home gardens. Late-ripening, large freestone variety produces lots of fruit. Cream-colored skin with red highlights; firm white flesh.

Nectarines <small>continued</small>

Dwarf Nectarines

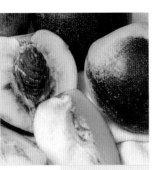

MERICREST

Hardy, disease-resistant, midseason freestone with bright red skin and yellow, flavorful flesh.

PANAMINT

Midseason freestone with medium to large fruit. Red skin and yellow flesh. Low-chill requirements.

SNOW QUEEN

Large nectarine; lightly colored with juicy white flesh. Ripens early.

NECTAR BABE

Genetic dwarf variety with small to medium-size freestone fruit, dark red skin, and yellow flesh. Ripens midseason.

NECTAR ZEE

(*or* 'Necta Zee') Earlier ripening genetic dwarf with medium-size fruits, red skin, and sweet yellow flesh.

SOUTHERN BELLE

Early-harvest dwarf variety with low-chill requirements. Fruit is large with yellow skin tinged with red and flavorful yellow flesh.

A backyard plum in flower; notice also the creative repurposing of an old wooden ladder as a grape trellis.

Plums and Prunes

Plums are incredibly versatile. Not only are they good fresh, cooked, canned, and, particularly in the case of prunes, dried, but they are great garden trees. Their white blossoms are wonderfully scented, and the fruit itself is colorful. There are, of course, the varieties with purple skin, but some varieties produce fruit that is red, yellow, peach-colored, green, and even blue to blue bordering on black. When you bite into a plum, the flesh color can also vary, ranging from yellow, to green, to red.

Plums are also less needy than their stone fruit cousins. They don't grow quite as vigorously as peaches and nectarines, so pruning is easier. They're better at handling drought, and although they can get fungal diseases and be bothered by pests, they're much less prone to these problems.

Prunes, that old standby from our grandparents, are making a comeback as people discover their sweet flavor and high nutritional value. Prunes are the dried fruits of certain very sweet European plums. The trick is to choose the right variety to get the best flavor. The fruit can be eaten fresh as well, but it can be too sweet for some people's taste.

> When you're shopping for plum trees, make sure you get edible varieties. Flowering varieties will produce lovely flowers and foliage, but no fruit.

CHOOSING A PLUM: THE BASICS

Plums come in three major types: Japanese (sometimes called Oriental), European, and hardy hybrids. Each type offers plenty of options, and good choices are available for almost any climate. Depending on what you plant, you can harvest plums from late spring through late summer, and possibly into early autumn. You won't find any true dwarf plum varieties, but some semi-dwarf trees are a bit smaller than the standard.

Japanese plums, such as 'Santa Rosa' and 'Satsuma', are the earliest bloomers and also sport the largest fruit. They have a softer skin and more juice than European and hardy hybrids. Eat them fresh off the tree to enjoy their taste, which is a bit more tart than that of other plums. Because they bloom early, they're not a great choice for areas with late spring frosts, but because they need less winter chill, they fare well in climates with warmer winters. Many Japanese plums need to be pollinated by another Japanese plum or a hybrid plum to produce fruit.

European plums, such as 'Green Gage' and 'Stanley', and the hybrid 'Damson' plum, are good choices for most home orchards. Because they bloom later than Japanese plums, they are the best option for areas with later winters and rainy springs. Many, but not all, European plums are self-fertile, although a second tree might be needed if fruit yield is small. They are generally both sweeter and firmer than Japanese plums. They can be eaten fresh but are also a good choice cooking and canning.

Hardy hybrids are bred for cold and windy areas, such as the northern Great Plains states and Canada. They're a blend of Japanese plums and wild plums and are often listed as Japanese-American hybrids or cherry-plum hybrids. They can be grown as small trees or even shrubs. Check with your local nursery for good pollinizers. Although they are ideal for harsher climates, these plums also do well in more moderate areas. In addition to the hardy hybrids, some plum hybrids are crosses with apricots and peaches.

If growing space is limited, look for varieties that are semi-dwarf and use summer pruning techniques to keep trees in check.

GROWING PLUMS

As with most fruit trees, plums do best if they grow in a sunny location. They also prefer well-drained soil, but they're more tolerant of less-than-ideal soil than many fruit trees. Japanese plums are best pruned to an open vase shape, so look for trees with strong lateral branches. For European plums, look for trees with a strong center trunk.

GETTING STARTED Plant bare-root trees in late winter or early spring, or plant them in the fall in areas with warmer winters. After the tree is planted, do a preliminary pruning to remove excess branches and begin to shape the tree. Be patient; plums can take up to five years before they start producing fruit.

GROWING SEASON CARE Regular moderate watering is essential for all plums. Set a watering schedule if spring and summer rains are inadequate, and mulch to conserve moisture. Mulch will also help prevent bruising when fruit begins to ripen and fall to the ground.

Both Japanese and European plums are heavy feeders. In early spring, feed trees with a balanced fertilizer, up to 10-10-10, for both healthy foliage and increased fruit size. To encourage foliage and fruit production, increase the nitrogen (the first number in the triad) slightly. Too much nitrogen, however, and you'll end up with lots of leaves and no fruit, so don't overdo it.

Generally, European and hardy hybrid plums do not require fruit thinning. Japanese plums can set a large amount of fruit. After the fruit begins to form, thin them to remove the excess, leaving about 6 inches between each fruit. You'll be guaranteed larger fruit and won't risk damaging thin branches with too much weight.

If your fruit is too heavy, the plum's somewhat fragile limbs can break. Keep an eye on the tree and support heavy branches with props until the crop is ready to pick.

HARVESTING The fruit on most plum trees tends to ripen all at once, so be ready for this when harvest season arrives. Japanese plums and late-bearing plums can be picked slightly firm and allowed to ripen. European plums should be picked when ripe, but they last longer on the tree.

Ripe fruit should be fully colored and somewhat soft when gently squeezed. Twist gently to remove the fruit from the branch; if it doesn't come off easily, wait until it is more ripe.

Ideally, you'll pick fruit before it falls, but don't overlook fruit that has fallen to the ground or even those that have been slightly pecked by birds or animals. It's easy to cut out bruised pieces and use the fruit for cooking and canning.

Plums will last for a few days after picking and for a couple of weeks if refrigerated. Late-bearing plums and those picked while still firm will last longer.

PRUNING

All plum trees require some shaping and pruning, if only to remove dead branches and keep trees at a reasonable size. Japanese plums require the most work, because they are vigorous growers and need to be kept in check for best fruit production.

An open vase shape is the best choice for Japanese plums. Fruit grows on short spurs and year-old branches of these varieties, so cut back branches to keep them closer to the trunk and to encourage spur growth and stronger limbs. The trees also like to grow upward, so keep this growth in check. If space is limited, or to provide more protection against frost, train Japanese plums in a fan shape against a wall.

European plums produce fruit on short spurs. They grow best when pruned to a central leader (a single vertical extension of the trunk from which all branches originate) with branches lightly pruned back.

Hardy hybrids need little pruning, especially if they are shrubby. For these types, cut older shoots to the ground every few years and clean out the center to allow better air circulation and fruit production.

PESTS AND DISEASES

Although subject to pests and diseases, plums tend to be much more problem-free than other stone fruits, and disease-resistant varieties are available. Brown rot is a problem in humid areas; spraying trees with horticultural oil during the dormant season will help control this disease as well as many insect pest problems. Stop the problem before it starts by disposing of diseased fruits.

Black knot, which produces warty, black galls on branches, can also be a problem in humid areas. Prevent it from spreading by removing all infected branches, cutting them off cleanly where they attach to an adjacent branch without leaving spurs.

One of the more problematic insect pests, especially in eastern parts of North America, is the plum curculio, a beetle that damages fruit. Small infestations can be handled using traps, but heavily infested trees can require preventive spraying. Spraying can also help with problems such as leafhoppers, canker (caused by a fungus), and mites. Borers can also infect trunks and branches, especially if the tree is already weak or damaged.

Birds are the most likely large pest you'll encounter in your plum trees. Hanging shiny objects and using fake predator birds (moved periodically so the pesky birds don't get used to them) can help. You can also try netting the tree, but be sure to tie off the netting firmly at the trunk and check to ensure that birds and other animals don't get trapped inside.

Japanese Plums

PLUM & PRUNE VARIETIES

Some plums are longtime favorites, but you'll find newer plum varieties that have been bred to fit specific needs. Check with your local nursery, cooperative extension, or other agricultural agency for the best varieties for your area. Or consider grafting two or three varieties to one rootstock or planting two or three trees in a single hole to extend the harvest season without taking up too much space.

AUTUMN ROSA

Sweet plum ripens late and can stay on the tree longer than most. Self-fertile; good low-chill choice. Fruit color from purple to red with yellow flesh.

BURBANK

Midseason plum. Large and relatively sweet, with red skin and yellow flesh. Needs a pollinizer. Handles cold better than most Japanese plums.

BURGUNDY

Small early plum. Self-fertile with low chill requirements. Dark red fruit has a strong flavor and can be eaten fresh or canned. Fruit can stay on the tree longer than most plums.

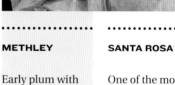

ELEPHANT HEART

Very large, deep red, heart-shaped fruit. Ripens midseason to late; needs a pollinizer. Wait until fully ripe to harvest; fruit can stay on tree longer than most plums.

HOWARD MIRACLE

Midseason plum with yellow skin with red overtones, yellow flesh, and a distinctive taste that's less sweet than other plums. Needs a pollinizer.

LATE SANTA ROSA

Medium-large plum ripens later than its 'Santa Rosa' parent. Purple fruit with yellow to red flesh. Self-fertile.

METHLEY

Early plum with low chill requirements and hardy blooms. Medium dark red skin and sweet flesh.

SANTA ROSA

One of the most well-known plum varieties. Self-fertile, early ripener is good for low-chill areas. Tart fruit is purple-red with yellow flesh. Remove skin before canning. Weeping variety is available.

Japanese Plums continued

European Plums

SATSUMA

Medium-size, deep red fruit with a small pit; perfect for preserves. Needs a pollinizer; ripens early. Also called blood plum.

SHIRO

Medium to large yellow plum ripens midseason. Abundant fruit can be eaten fresh or canned. Self-fertile.

BAVAY'S GREEN GAGE

(*or* 'Reine Claude de Bavay') Large fruit on a small tree. Skin is yellow with white spots; flesh is yellow, similar in taste to 'Green Gage'. Self-fertile, late ripener, and available as a dwarf.

BROOKS

Sweet, large midseason prune plum for the Pacific Northwest. Self-fertile. Fruit has yellow to blue skin with yellow flesh that is fairly sweet. Good choice for canning or drying.

COE'S GOLDEN DROP

Late season fruit with intense flavor. Needs pollinizer.

DAMSON AND VARIETIES

('French Damson', 'Blue Damson', 'Shropshire Damson') Technically a hybrid. Small, tart fruit with almost black skin and green flesh that ripens late. Self-fertile. Good for low-chill areas.

FRENCH PRUNE

Small, late fruit with red to purple skin and yellow flesh tinged with green. Self-fertile. Very sweet. Common for drying.

GREEN GAGE

Old variety of midseason plum. Reddish skin with sweet yellow-gold flesh. Self-fertile. Use fresh or in cooked dishes; good for canning and preserves.

IMPERIAL

Midseason to late, large purple fruit with very sweet yellow-green flesh. Needs a pollinizer. Excellent fresh, dried, or canned.

SENECA

Large, late-ripening, oblong red fruit with sweet yellow flesh. Needs a pollinizer. Good for eating fresh.

STANLEY

Very popular plum, especially in the U.S. Midwest, South, and East, and in parts of Canada. Highly productive tree, medium to large purple fruit with yellow flesh. Ripens midseason. Self-fertile. Good fresh, cooked, or canned.

Hardy Plums

OPATA

Cherry-plum hybrid shrub. Small purple fruit with sweet green flesh. Ripens late. Needs a pollinizer. Eat fresh or use for preserves.

PIPESTONE

Large Japanese-American variety that ripens midseason. Red skin and yellow flesh. Good for eating fresh and for jams and jellies. Very hardy and doesn't need much summer heat. Needs a pollinizer.

SAPALTA

Cherry-plum hybrid shrub. Small all-around fruit with red-purple skin and dark flesh. Mildly sweet. Ripens late. Needs a pollinizer.

SUPERIOR

Large gold fruit with yellow flesh. Ripens late midseason. Best for jams and jellies. Hardy; needs a pollinizer.

UNDERWOOD

Hardy plum; great for eating and jams. Medium-size, dark red skin with gold flesh; fruit ripens early.

Apriums, Plumcots, Pluots, and Interspecific Crosses

Chance hybrids of plums and other stone fruits are likely to have occurred since these trees were first cultivated. But to modern gardeners and cooks, plum hybrids are specific crosses created by plant breeders. These modern hybrids got their start more than 100 years ago, when Luther Burbank developed the first plum-apricot hybrid. Since then, more and more crosses between plums and apricots and recently between plums and peaches have been developed.

Fortunately, supermarkets, grocery stores, and farmers' markets often carry these hybrids, so you can taste-test the difference between varieties before choosing a tree for your own garden. As for growing them, most plum hybrids require the same conditions as their dominant parents, including winter chill. If you can grow a plum tree, you can grow plumcots and pluots. Apriums require the same growing conditions as apricots; peach-plum and nectarine-plum hybrids do well in areas where peaches thrive.

CHOOSING A HYBRID: THE BASICS

The first plum-apricot cross developed for today's market was the plumcot. Usually about half apricot and half plum, plumcots resemble their plum parents in looks, with very smooth skin and a slightly sweeter taste. Trees are usually self-fertile, but it can take several years before they produce fruit.

Pluots generally have more plum than apricot in their mix and can be grown in areas where 'Santa Rosa' plums thrive. They often require a pollinizer, either another pluot or a Japanese plum. Although the name *Pluot* is the trademark for varieties developed by breeder Floyd Zeiger, it is often used as a general term for any plum-apricot cross that owes more to its plum parent than the apricot one. As a result, you should check that you're getting exactly the pluot you want.

Both plumcots and pluots are very sweet, flavorful, and juicy. They're usually about 2 to 3 inches in size. Color ranges from deep purple or red to lighter red and yellow, depending on the variety.

Apriums taste more like their apricot parent with just a hint of plum. The small, yellow fruit also reflects the apricot heritage. The fruit ripens relatively early, in spring or early summer. Trees do best with a pollinizer, either 'Flavor Supreme' pluot or an apricot.

The newest additions to the plum-hybrid family are peach-plum and nectarine-plum crosses. These trees are fairly new on the scene, so finding them can be difficult but well worth the effort.

GROWING HYBRIDS

Plum hybrids are like other fruit trees—they want a warm, sunny spot with good, well-drained soil. The trees that owe more to their plum parents can probably handle more diverse conditions, while those more like their apricot parents will be more cold hardy. In all cases, check to see what will grow well in your area before you plant.

GETTING STARTED Plant bare-root trees in late winter or early spring, as soon as the ground can be worked. Trees in containers can be planted from fall through spring; avoid planting in the heat of summer. After the tree is planted, lightly prune to shape it; you'll probably want to create an open vase shape for the best air circulation.

GROWING SEASON CARE Trees do best with moderate but consistent watering throughout the growing season. To help conserve water and inhibit weeds, spread mulch around the tree, keeping it about 3 inches away from the trunk. Plum hybrids aren't heavy feeders, but you should provide a balanced fertilizer in early spring before the tree leafs out.

After the trees start bearing, you might need to thin the young fruits. Not only can too many fruits break limbs, but a heavy crop one year is often followed by a very light one the next. Thinning keeps crops more consistent from year to year.

HARVESTING Depending on the variety, plum hybrid fruits can be picked from spring through fall. In all cases, the fruit should be fully colored with no green showing and slightly soft to the touch when gently squeezed (use your palm to avoid bruising). The best indicator is taste; wait to pick the fruit until it is fully ripe.

PRUNING

Prune trees during the dormant season to remove damaged, diseased, and crossing branches and to maintain the tree shape. Then follow the pruning instructions for the dominant parent tree. Tree height generally ranges from 10 to 20 feet. Prune in summer and during the dormant season to keep the tree at the smaller size to make it easier to access the fruit.

PESTS AND DISEASES

Plum hybrids are no more immune to disease and pest problems than their parents, so good orchard sanitation practices are important to tree health. Remove and destroy diseased fruit and branches, and pick up fallen fruit. Sanitize your garden equipment to prevent diseases from spreading through contact. Remove weeds growing around the trees.

Brown rot and gummosis are the most likely problems

you'll encounter with plum hybrids. Brown rot symptoms include cracking and oozing wood and branches and fruit with brownish circular discoloration. When brown rot appears, dispose of the affected fruit. Spray with lime sulfur (not horticultural oil) prebloom to prevent a return.

Gummosis is a general term for gummy substances oozing out of cracks in the tree. The cause can be anything from a damaged branch, to peach tree borers, to a canker infestation. A healthy tree is less likely to succumb to this. For treatment, first identify the underlying cause; your local nursery, cooperative extension service, or other agricultural agency can be helpful.

Peach and nectarine crosses can also be affected by peach leaf curl. The best prevention is a spraying regimen beginning in the fall and continuing until late winter or early spring. After the disease appears, it is too late to do anything about it for the current season.

For animal pests such as birds and squirrels, netting is probably the best choice, although you should make sure that animals don't get caught under the net. Hanging shining objects in the trees or installing fake predators (move them periodically) might also help deter birds and squirrels.

Apriums

HYBRID VARIETIES

Choices among the plum hybrids are rapidly increasing as breeders create more and more varieties. Some of the most popular and successful selections, as well as some of the newer ones, are listed.

COT-N-CANDY

Resembles an apricot, with very sweet, white flesh. Ripens in late spring or early summer. Self-fertile.

FLAVOR DELIGHT

Resembles its apricot parent and tastes much the same with just a hint of plum. Ripens in late spring. Produces best with a pollinizer.

Plumcots

Pluots

FLAVORELLA

Medium-sized fruit with golden skin and firm, sweet-tart flesh. Ripens in late spring or early summer. Low chill requirements. Needs a pollinizer.

PLUM PARFAIT

A classic choice. Ripens in late spring or early summer. Fruit is marbled pink; flavor is a wonderful combination of sweet and tart. The tree is slow to mature and smaller than either of its parents. Self-fertile.

DAPPLE DANDY

(*or* 'Dinosaur Egg') Large, fairly firm fruit with yellowish skin tinged with red. White flesh with red streaks. Fruit ripens midseason. Good pollinizer for other pluots, but is not self-fertile.

FLAVOR GRENADE

Large green fruit with hints of red; more oblong than round in shape. Flesh is yellow and juicy. Ripens in late summer, but can stay on the tree longer in mild climates. Needs a pollinizer.

FLAVOR KING

Late-season pluot with distinctive purplish skin and purple-red flesh. Fruit must ripen completely before flesh softens; the result is a juicy, fruit-mix sweetness. Smaller than its parent trees. Needs a pollinizer.

FLAVOR QUEEN

Medium to large fruit ripens from midsummer to late summer. Can remain on tree after ripe. Yellow-green skin, with sweet and juicy yellow flesh. Needs a pollinizer.

Pluots continued

Interspecific Crosses

FLAVOR SUPREME

Medium to medium-large fruit with greenish skin dappled in red and juicy red flesh. Early ripener. Good pollinizer for other pluots.

FLAVOROSA

Early summer dark purple fruit with sweet, red flesh. Good pollinizer for 'Flavorella'.

SPLASH

Early ripener. Yellow-orange flesh tinged with red. Skin can be yellow, orange, or red. Very sweet. Smaller than parent trees. Needs a pollinizer.

SPICE ZEE

Nectarine-plum (nectaplum) hybrid with red skin and yellow flesh. Good blend of flavors from both parents. Self-fertile; ripens late.

TRI-LITE

Peach-plum hybrid that ripens early. Skin is red with white flesh. Mild peach flavored with a hint of plum. Self-fertile.

Apricots

Apricots are the most delicate of the stone fruits. Because they bruise easily, they don't hold as well for shipping or last long in the produce section. Having your own tree ensures that you'll be able to enjoy their goodness at the peak of the season. As if they weren't delicious enough when fresh, apricots have long been used for jams, preserves, and baking, and they are increasingly being used in drinks, salads, and entrées. Extend the season by drying the fruit for a great year-round treat.

Apricots also make great landscape trees. They're not too large; standard trees are 15 to 20 feet tall and genetic dwarf trees top out at around 8 feet. Their pink or white blossoms are produced in early spring, which can make them more likely to be damaged by frosts, but having early color in the garden is worth the risk. The foliage is bronze when it first appears and becomes dark green as it matures. After you harvest the fruit, an apricot makes an excellent landscape tree that provides great shade throughout the summer.

Apricots originated in Asia and are a staple of Middle Eastern cuisine. English settlers are thought to have brought the trees to North America's East Coast, and Spanish missionaries brought them to Mexico and the American West. George Washington reported on his success in growing them at Mount Vernon. Today, almost all commercial apricots sold in North America are grown in California, but they can be grown elsewhere, especially in areas with temperate climates and where problem pests and diseases aren't prevalent.

CHOOSING AN APRICOT: THE BASICS

Apricots can tolerate cold temperatures, unlike some of the other stone fruits such as peaches. But they flower so early that frosts can destroy the blossoms and any hope of fruit. After they've blossomed, they want dry weather, so overly wet springs can also wreak havoc on the crop. If you want to try growing apricots in a questionable climate, check with local nurseries, the cooperative extension service, or another local

Soft foliage, a graceful form, and distinctive bark make the apricot a great landscape tree.

agricultural resource; they can tell you whether the danger of frost is too intense in colder climates and recommend low-chill varieties in areas with mild winters. Most apricots are self-fertile, but often adding a second tree for cross-pollination will help with fruit production.

GROWING APRICOTS

Apricots do best in fairly light, well-drained soil, in a sunny spot that is sheltered from cold winds or cold spots during the bloom time. Unlike other stone fruit trees, apricots do not grow very tall, and some dwarf varieties can be grown in containers.

GETTING STARTED Bare-root apricot trees are probably the most common types sold in nurseries. In most areas, plant them in late winter or early spring, as soon as the ground can be worked and frosts are no longer expected. You can also plant trees in fall in milder climates. Try to avoid planting in areas where you've grown tomatoes, eggplants, or other plants subject to verticillium wilt, because this disease remains in the soil and can infect apricots.

GROWING SEASON CARE Water trees regularly from the time blooms appear until you harvest the fruit. Water deeply, two or three times per week, rather than relying on daily shallow watering; adding mulch around the tree (keeping it 3 inches away from the trunk) will help the soil retain water. Keep the ground and mulch under the tree relatively soft and smooth to help avoid bruising fallen fruit. After you've picked all the fruit, cut back on the water, but don't stop watering until after all leaves have fallen.

Apricots require little fertilizer. Feed with a low-nitrogen formula in spring. You might need to fertilize container-grown plants throughout the growing season; monitor their progress.

Fruit can be thinned as it matures, about halfway between the time fruit begins to form and when its time to harvest. This helps to avoid excessive drop at the end of the season and produces larger fruits. Leave 2 to 4 inches of space between each fruit.

HARVESTING Apricots ripen in early to midsummer, depending on the variety. The fruit is ripe when it is fully orange in color and slightly soft to the touch. To harvest, gently twist the fruit from the tree. Apricots won't last long on or off the tree, so plan to use them as soon as possible.

PRUNING

Newly planted apricots can be trained as either an open vase shape or with a modified leader. As they grow, apricots require more maintenance pruning than strong shaping. Fruit forms on spurs on the previous year's growth and are usually productive for a few years. To encourage better fruiting, cut out spurs that are no longer producing. Although pruning during the dormant season is usually standard practice for most fruit trees, you should prune apricots in the summer after you've harvested the fruit. This prevents diseases that spread during rainy weather from entering the cuts and weakening the tree. If a tree gets too large, summer pruning will help keep the size in check.

Apricots can also be espaliered. Training against a sunny wall can be a good idea if you live in an area subject to chills or frosts during blossom time, as the reflected heat from the wall can help protect the tree.

PESTS AND DISEASES

Depending on your location, apricots do not require as much seasonal care as many other fruit trees, but they are susceptible to some diseases and pests. To help prevent these problems, keep the area around the tree free of weeds, fallen fruit, diseased branches and leaves, and other debris. Clean and disinfect garden tools before using them on the tree to prevent diseases from spreading through cuts and care. If particular diseases are prevalent in your area, look for resistant apricot varieties.

Brown rot can be a problem especially in wet climates. It begins with browned blossoms and leaves and can result in oozing branches, powdery fungus, and darkened and shriveled fruits. Other fungal diseases include black knot, leaf spot, and powdery mildew. Apricots are also subject to silver leaf and cankers.

Nematodes and aphids can also bother your apricots. You might open up an apricot and find a worm inside. Because of this, many home apricot growers recommend twisting the fruit open and checking first rather than biting into the whole fruit.

You can try a number of solutions to handle these problems, but most involve a preventive spray schedule. Products and timing vary depending on the pest and disease, so check with nurseries and your local cooperative extension or other agricultural agency to determine your best course of action.

Squirrels and birds can also decimate much of the crop, usually just before the fruit ripens. Try netting the tree to prevent birds from reaching the fruit (take care that animals don't get caught in nets) or hanging shiny objects in the tree to scare away animals. Squirrels are the bane of most apricot growers. Setting out fake predators can help, as can the presence of the family cat or dog.

Apricots

APRICOT VARIETIES

Everyone is familiar with a few traditional popular apricot varieties, such as 'Blenheim' and 'Stanley', but many selections are available for home orchards. Dwarf apricots are also available, although they are rare. Most apricot trees are relatively small, so a standard size with pruning can work well in a small garden.

AUTUMN GLO

Great flavor; ripens in late summer.

AUTUMN ROYAL

The latest ripening apricot, with fruit ready in the early autumn. Self-fertile.

Apricots *continued*

BLENHEIM

(*or* 'Royal') Classic California apricot. Can be canned or dried. Ripens early to midseason. Self-fertile.

FLORA GOLD

Natural semi-dwarf with full-size fruit. Ripens early. Self-fruitful.

GOLD KIST

Good mild-winter apricot with a slightly more tart flavor than most. Ripens early. Self-fruitful.

GOLDCOT

Midseason apricot with a sweet flavor; does well in cold climates.

HARCOT

Very juicy, early apricot with medium to large fruit. Good for areas with late frosts. Self-fertile.

MANCHURIAN BUSH

(*Prunus armeniaca* var. *mandshurica*) Grown as a shrub or a small tree. Ripens mid-summer with small orange fruit that can be dried. Hardy. Self-fertile.

MONTROSE

Hardy variety named for its Colorado home. Large, sweet fruit ripens late.

MOONGOLD

Large fruit ripens midsummer to late summer. Good for areas with cold winters. Needs 'Sungold' as a pollinizer.

MOORPARK

Popular apricot with large fruit; ripens midsummer. Great for eating or drying; not good for canning. Self-fertile.

NEWCASTLE

Small midseason fruit that is sweet and juicy. Low-chill variety.

NUGGET

Heirloom freestone with flavorful yellow flesh. Vigorous, productive tree with some brown rot resistance. Self-fertile with low chill requirements.

Apricots _{continued}

PIXIE-COT

Genetic dwarf with medium fruit. Ripens early.

PUGET GOLD

Medium-size fruit ripens midseason. Disease resistant. Washington State University introduction; good choice for the Puget Sound area and southwestern Canada. Self-fertile.

ROYALTY

Very large fruit even when tree is young. Good for windy areas. Ripens early summer.

SUNGOLD

Large, slightly less round, bright orange fruit. Ripens early. Good for climates with cold winters. Needs 'Moongold' as a pollinizer.

WENATCHEE

(*or* 'Wenatchee Moorpark') Very large, flavorful fruit in midseason. Self-fertile, but having another variety nearby can be helpful if fruit set is consistently light.

Cherries

Cherries are the smallest, but probably one of the most universally popular, stone fruits. Although they are not the first to blossom (apricots claim that title), cherries are the generally the first to bear fruit, usually less than three months after their blossoms appear.

Like other stone fruits, cherries originated in Asia, were cultivated by the Greeks, and then spread throughout Europe. They were brought to North America by both British settlers and Spanish missionaries. Cherries of some sort can be grown throughout most of North America and have remained perennially popular in the United States. Children grow up knowing the story of George Washington chopping down a cherry tree, and cherry pie is a classic American dessert.

Cherry trees definitely stand out in the home garden, with their beautiful blossoms, reddish brown bark, serrated leaves, bright fruit, and colorful fall foliage. After harvesting the fruit, sit in the shade under this wonderful, spreading tree that can live for decades.

CHOOSING A CHERRY: THE BASICS

There are two main types of cherries: sweet and sour. Sweet cherries (*Prunus avium*) can be eaten out of hand. They are generally grown in western North America, especially along the Pacific coast, and in northern Michigan and Ontario. Some sweet cherries are self-fertile, but most are not, which means you'll likely need a second tree to ensure fruit set. Cherries are fussy—only certain varieties will pollinize other varieties. Check with a nursery, cooperative extension, or other agency to be sure the trees you're planting will cross-pollinate.

Standard sweet cherry trees can grow quite large, up to 50 feet. For home gardens, look for cherries that are grown on dwarfing rootstocks, especially if you are planting two trees. Even these trees can reach up to 20 feet. If space is limited in your garden, try to convince a neighbor to plant a cherry as well. You'll both benefit.

Sour or tart cherries (*Prunus cerasus*) can be grown across a good portion of North America. The fruit is usually too tart for

Farmers' market cherries for sale

In Japan, the blossoming of the cherry trees is cause for celebration. Naturally.

eating fresh, although some varieties are sweet enough to eat off the tree. Great for baking and jams, sour cherries are well worth planting if you like to cook with and preserve fruit. You'll just have to rely on grocers for a sweet cherry fix. Sour cherries also tend to be smaller than sweet cherries, reaching 15 to 20 feet, and they're also more likely to be self-fertile.

GROWING CHERRIES

Sweet cherries prefer well-draining soil and have specific climate requirements. They need a certain number of hours with temperatures below 45°F every winter (low-chill varieties are also available). At the same time, they don't do well in intense cold, nor do they thrive if summer months are too hot. Too much rain during the growing season can also harm or destroy developing fruit, and late frosts can destroy blossoms. You cannot prevent a badly timed frost, but if your area is prone to cold snaps late in the spring, try to plant your trees away from low-lying areas where cold air can pool.

Sour cherries are much more adaptable to a variety of soils and climates, as indicated by their wider range. Check with local experts to find trees for your area. Unfortunately, sour cherries generally will not pollinate sweet cherries; otherwise, planting both types would be a great choice for the home orchard.

GETTING STARTED When choosing a sweet cherry, look for trees with a strong central leader, strong limbs, and a good general shape. Sour cherries can be trained to a central leader or an open vase shape.

Plant bare-root cherries in late winter or early spring, after the ground can be worked and frosts are no longer expected. Container-grown or balled-and-burlapped trees can be planted in the fall, but if your area is prone to extreme cold, you might wait for spring. Plant trees in a spot that gets full sun and is not subject to cold air pooling.

Regular, well-drained soil is best for sweet cherries; add amendments before planting if you have heavy clay or sandy soil, and avoid places where the roots will remain wet. Sour cherries can handle less ideal soil. Try to avoid planting these trees in lawns, however; although older cherries can handle

encroaching grass, young trees are stressed by the conflicting watering needs of a lawn. When planting either type of cherry, keep the bud union (the graft junction) above the ground a minimum of 2 inches and preferably up to 5 inches.

GROWING SEASON CARE A regular watering schedule throughout most of the growing season is essential for cherries. Keep it steady and even until about two weeks before the fruit ripens. At that point, cut back on the amount of water you provide so the fruit won't split. Mulching will help retain water and discourage weeds, but keep any mulch at least 3 inches away from the trunk.

Cherries need surprisingly little fertilizer. In fact, sour cherries do well without any soil amendments. If sweet cherries are producing fruit every year, the soil around them usually doesn't need additional feeding. If fruit production is poor, add a balanced (10-10-10) fertilizer in the spring. For dwarf varieties, plan on using about ½ pound of tree fertilizer for each inch of trunk diameter. Use the same proportion for young standard trees and about 5 pounds total for mature standard trees.

HARVESTING Wait until cherries are completely ripe before you harvest, because they won't ripen after they've been picked. Plan to use them right away; they can quickly get mushy or moldy. Harvest by gently twisting the top of the stem, being careful not to damage the spur from which the cherry is growing. If your crop is large, consider freezing or drying the fruit. Dried cherries are appealingly sweet.

PRUNING

Cherries need relatively little pruning compared to some of the other stone fruits. In fact, the fruit on sweet cherries forms on spurs that develop on older wood, so they should be pruned only to remove dead or diseased branches, to shape the tree, and to keep the fruit within bounds for easy picking. Unlike many other trees, you should prune cherries just after the harvest rather than in the dormant season. Sweet cherries can be pruned to an open vase shape, but many trees have a strong central leader, and it's okay to retain the leader. Retain strong lateral branches, leaving about 2 feet between each succeeding branch, to encourage fruit production throughout the tree.

Sour cherries fruit on shoots from older wood. Prune to remove any dead or diseased branches, prune back longer branches, and remove the oldest wood that is no longer fruitful. Sour cherries also do well espaliered as a fan shape, especially against a wall.

Over the years, cherries can become large, spreading trees. To keep the fruit within reach, incorporate summer pruning into your care program after the tree reaches maturity.

PESTS AND DISEASES

Birds are the biggest problem for cherry growers. Netting the tree is probably the best solution, but keep watch so that birds and other animals don't get stuck under the netting. Birds seem to ignore yellow cherries, so if you're growing a yellow variety, your tree might be safe.

Other pests include scale, mites, aphids, and maggots, but these usually don't pose significant problems. A horticultural spray when the tree is dormant will control scale and mites. You might need to turn to insecticides for aphids and maggots. Borers, which produce holes in the trunk followed by oozing sap, are best prevented by maintaining a clean garden and making sure the trunk is not damaged and the tree is generally in good shape. Borers can also respond to an insecticide; consult an expert if the infestation is large.

Diseases can be more problematic than insects—from brown rot and blossom blight, to black knot and powdery mildew. Brown rot and blossom blight causes flower wilt, grayish spores on young branches, and rotted fruit that eventually mummifies. To prevent these diseases, apply a copper spray in the fall and then again in the spring, first when blooms appear and then again two weeks before harvest.

Black knot starts on the newest branches and can be identified by brown swellings that grow and split. Powdery mildew, a common plant problem, is particularly prevalent in areas with high humidity. You'll notice white patches and leaves that are disfigured and dropping. White patches can also be a sign of cherry leaf spot, but the first symptoms are usually dark spots on the leaves and leaf drop. Spraying with a fungicide as well as removing all affected branches and leaves will help control all three of these problems.

Another fungal problem, silver leaf, can be diagnosed by the appearance of silvery leaves or leaves turning brown, and also by twigs and branches dying. Remove affected branches and dispose of them; no controls are available.

Garden sanitation is the first step in preventing or reducing most of these problems. Keep your orchard free of garden debris, dispose of fallen and diseased fruit, and remove diseased or damaged limbs.

A backyard sweet cherry does a lovely job of making an otherwise unused corner quite fruitful.

Sweet Cherries

CHERRY VARIETIES

The number of sweet cherries available to home gardeners is growing rapidly. Although the cherry season is relatively short, you'll find early, midseason, and late season cherries for your orchard.

BING

The standard-bearer for sweet cherries. Ripens midseason, with large, dark red fruit. Prone to splitting.

BLACK TARTARIAN

Early cherry that is small and sweet. Prone to cracking. Good pollinizer.

CRAIG'S CRIMSON

Natural dwarf, but needs some pruning to retain small size. Medium-size, deep red fruit in midseason. Self-fertile.

KRISTIN

Very hardy, midseason cherry with large, black fruit. Not prone to cracking.

LAMBERT

Late producer with large black-red fruit.

LAPINS

Early to midseason fruit, similar to 'Bing', but self-fertile.

Sweet Cherries continued

RAINIER

Yellow cherry that ripens midseason. Frost-hardy. Less susceptible to bird damage.

ROYAL ANN

Large tree. Midseason, tender, light yellow cherry. Sometimes sold as 'Napoleon'.

STELLA

Late cherry with dark fruit. Self-fertile. 'Compact Stella' is a dwarf variety.

SWEETHEART

Late cherry with bright red fruit with strong cherry flavor. Self-fertile.

VAN

Heavy producer. Ripens early to midseason with medium-size black fruit.

Sour Cherries

EARLY RICHMOND

Early cherry with small, red fruit. Sweet-tart flavor; very juicy.

ENGLISH MORELLO

Late cherry with dark, tart fruit. Good for jams and pies.

METEOR

Late cherry with small, bright red fruit. Naturally semi-dwarf, tree tends to top off naturally at 12 feet.

MONTMORENCY

Midseason to late cherry with small, firm, tangy, red fruit. Considered the standard sour cherry for pies.

NORTH STAR

Firm midseason cherry with deep red skin and yellow, tangy flesh. Natural dwarf.

Pome FRUiTS

In the orchard family album, the pome family of fruits isn't as varied as the stone family, but you still have a lot of options. Apples and pears are the key members of the pome fruit family, and the number of available selections for North American gardeners is almost

Who wouldn't be tempted to bite into one of these apples?

staggering. Both apple and pear trees can grow in a surprisingly wide range of climates. They can become prominent features of a landscape or simply small trees set in containers. They provide fruit from summer through fall, and if the fruit isn't eaten fresh, it can be used in any number of cooked and baked dishes or preserved in a variety of ways.

A third member of the pome family shouldn't be overlooked in a home orchard. That's the quince. Although it's not quite as versatile as its apple and pear cousins, it's still a worthy addition to any cook's kitchen and a lovely addition to the garden.

Pome fruits all have a core with several small pockets for seeds, surrounded by a thick, fleshy layer. What's important to the gardener isn't the definition, but the trees themselves. They can be very hardy; apple trees have been surviving for decades in some of the most unexpected places. They can also be problematic; their resistance to disease varies by variety and can be quite poor. But with careful selection, and by paying attention to their needs, you'll enjoy a homegrown crop of apples, pears, and quinces for years.

Because of their popularity, you'll find many selections at local nurseries as well as mail-order sources. Some favorites are grafted onto semi-dwarf or dwarfing rootstocks, and some genetic dwarf trees are also available. For gardens large or small, if you want to grow apples, pears, and quince, you should find something to fit your needs.

Apples

Who doesn't like apples? They are found in pies and lunchboxes everywhere. Apples are a great snacking food, but they also find their way into a number of dishes, from breakfast pancakes to dessert crisps. Dry them, turn them into jams and jellies, create preserves and sauces, or squeeze them for juice or cider. In fact, apples might be one of the most versatile, and best loved, fruits around.

One thing you don't have to worry about if you're considering planting an apple tree is lack of variety. You'll find apple selections that grow everywhere from the coldest northern plains and valleys to the mild climates of the American Southwest; the only places they don't grow are in the warmest tropical and subtropical climates. Some apples ripen as early as midsummer and some will still be ripening in late autumn.

Apples also make great landscape trees. They start the growing season with pink or white blossoms that fill the air with their fragrant scent. Come summer, a standard apple's branches provide shade, and dwarf apples provide a colorful garden accent.

CHOOSING AN APPLE: THE BASICS

Because of the sheer number of varieties available, choosing the best one can seem daunting. If you're buying from a local nursery, you should find selections that will perform well in your growing conditions. If you're buying from a mail-order source, double check recommended climate zones and growing conditions as well as resistance to diseases.

Even though apples grow throughout North America, climate is still one of the most important considerations when you're choosing a specific variety. Different varieties need varying amounts of winter chill. In addition, apples grown in the coldest climates require the appropriate rootstock to withstand harsh winter conditions. Apples also can be highly susceptible to diseases; choosing resistant varieties will ensure that apples develop well and the tree survives.

A beautiful red apple

A dwarf apple hides a number of nearly ripe fruits.

ALTERNATIVES TO TWO TREES

Some fruit tree growers have managed to cross-pollinate a tree by setting a bucket filled with flowering branches from another tree that is a pollinizer on the ground nearby. Another option is to plant a tree with several apple varieties grafted on one rootstock. This gives you two additional advantages: multiple apples in one space as well as (with the right choices) ripe apples from summer into fall. If you have planted a single-variety apple tree, you can graft on one or more additional varieties for pollination and extended harvest. Also consider planting two, three, or four trees, spaced 18 inches apart, in a single planting hole.

Another consideration is pollination. In urban or suburban areas, viable pollen sources will likely be available within the couple of miles that bees travel. If a tree doesn't produce much fruit, remember that although some apples are fairly self-fertile, others need another apple in the area for cross-pollination and to set fruit. Some apple varieties, including 'Gravenstein', 'Mutsu', and 'Jonagold', tend to grow large with large fruit and require cross-pollination. Your best bet is to plant more than one tree.

Tree size is another important consideration. A standard apple tree usually reaches at least 20 feet tall and is equally as wide, and often even larger; you can, as the song says, sit under it. For most home gardens, however, smaller trees are more appropriate. Fortunately, many small tree selections are available, whether they are naturally smaller or have been grafted onto dwarfing rootstock.

Spur apples, for example, which produce fruit on short branches, are naturally about a third smaller than standard apples and can be grafted onto rootstocks that further reduce

their size. Semi-dwarf apples are about half the size of a standard tree and can be espaliered or grown as a hedge. Dwarf apples reach 8 feet tall and wide and require auxiliary support and training. Most are grown on dwarfing rootstocks, although 'Golden Delicious' is an example of a naturally small tree. Dwarf apples also produce fruit earlier than standard trees.

Another form for a small garden is a column-style or colonnade tree, which grows to about 8 feet tall but not wider than 2 feet. These trees can be grown in containers. They almost always need another apple for cross-pollination, so plan on planting at least two trees.

Your most important decision probably concerns which apple you like to eat. Do you want crisp and tart? Soft and sweet? Some apples are best for eating fresh and others are better for cooking. Some can be used for both. Keep in mind that the fruit you find in the local grocery store might not be the best fruiting tree in your area; check the farmers' market to be sure you're planting a variety that will grow best in your garden.

GROWING APPLES

Apple trees are sold as either bare-root or container plants. For most trees, look for plants with strong side branches that are widely angled and circle the tree. For columnar apple trees, look for trees with evenly spaced side branches.

GETTING STARTED Choose a spot in full sun with well-drained soil. Even though apples need chill, don't plant the tree in a low-lying area where cold air can pool and a spring frost can damage blossoms. Most trees can handle less than ideal soil, but fruit production can suffer.

Plant bare-root trees in late winter or early spring, as soon as the soil can be worked. Container-grown trees can be planted year-round, provided the soil is workable and not too cold. During an extremely cold winter, you should wait until temperatures warm a bit to give the tree a better start. After planting, do some light pruning to remove any weak or crossing branches and to help keep even a standard tree to a smaller size for easier fruit access. If you're planning to espalier the tree or use it as a hedge, start the training process now by pruning to keep only the strongest branches in the best location on the trunk to achieve that final goal. If no acceptable branches present themselves, cut back the trunk just above your first trellis wire; new branches will form near that cut.

Plant standard apple trees 20 to 30 feet apart. Spur apples and semi-dwarf apples can be planted 12 to 16 feet apart, and dwarf apples should be 5 to 8 feet apart. Allow at least 18 inches between columnar apple trees or multiple plantings in a single hole.

Dwarf apples have shallow roots, and the trees need support by staking or trellising, or by growing them against a fence or wall. Set up the basics of a support system when you plant the tree.

GROWING SEASON CARE After trees are in the ground, keep them well watered. If rainfall is insufficient, provide water. The soil shouldn't be soggy, but the top 12 inches should be kept moist. Water less often but deeply, especially for smaller trees; light waterings encourage even more shallow roots.

Mulching will not only help the soil retain moisture, but it will discourage weeds and keep the ground soft. Use organic mulch, spreading it about 2 inches deep, starting about 3 inches from the trunk and extending to the edges, or drip line, of the young tree's canopy.

Begin fertilizing trees when the buds first open, using about ¼ pound of a balanced fertilizer. Continue this regimen, adding ¼ pound each year for the next few years until the trees are fully mature—eight or nine years for dwarf and column-type trees and later for other trees. In general, you should feed semi-dwarf and spur trees about 5 pounds of fertilizer per year and feed standards about 10 pounds. But don't just go by the numbers. You don't need to feed at all if the trees are producing annual growth of about 6 inches at the tips. And if the tree is producing excessive leaf growth and not as much fruit, cut back on the nitrogen.

Check on the fruit as it develops. Although apples often drop some fruit in early summer, additional thinning is a good idea, especially if the amount of heavy fruit threatens to break smaller branches. Thinning will also help the tree produce larger fruit. Don't go overboard on pruning to increase fruit size, however;

A fruit picker is a handy tool for tall trees.

smaller apples can be just as tasty (and easier to finish eating) than overly large fruit. In general, thin to keep remaining fruit about 8 to 10 inches apart. Another reason to thin: bearing a heavy crop one year can often lead to a smaller crop the next year. Thinning will keep the crop consistent from year to year.

If you are growing apples in a container and you live in a climate with cold winters, you should protect the trees' roots. The best bet is to move containers to a cool and sheltered spot if the temperature is dropping below 20°F.

HARVESTING For harvesting purposes, apples ripen at three times: early, midseason, and late. That means you might have apples as early as midsummer or as late as mid- to late autumn. Generally, early apples are ideal for eating or using immediately. Late apples often can be stored for longer periods. When the fruit looks ripe, pull off an apple and taste it. Depending on the variety, you might be able to leave the apples on the tree for a while. Most early apples, however, need to be harvested relatively quickly after they ripen to maintain their flavor and texture.

To harvest an apple, gently twist the stem while cradling the fruit, leaving intact the branch or spur on which it's growing. Store apples in a cool, dark place; for best results, wrap each fruit in paper.

PRUNING

Pruning an apple tree correctly is essential for strong trees and good fruit production. This will be your main chore for the first few years; most apples don't produce fruit immediately. Prune trees at the end of the dormant season; remove suckers (tall shoots emanating from the roots) and water sprouts (tall shoots growing from other parts of the tree) at any time.

When the tree is young, prune to encourage a modified leader shape. The primary branches should evenly circle the main trunk. Remove branches with narrow angles between the trunk and branch, and prune back any secondary branches that are outgrowing the leader and primary branches.

As the trees mature, remove any dead, diseased, disfigured, or crossing branches and any new growth that does not conform to the overall shape of the tree. It's also a good idea to remove most new interior branches: a more open tree allows air to circulate through the leaves and helps prevent disease. Branches can continue to produce fruit for up to 20 years, so don't worry that you'll lessen fruit production if you remove a good deal of new growth. Do leave some new growth, however, because the tree will grow more fruit if you periodically remove the oldest branches as they age. It's an imprecise balancing act, but never fear, because you'll likely have more than enough fruit if you shape the tree annually.

Dwarf trees can be trained along a wall or trellis in any number of traditional espalier patterns. They can also be grown as a long-living fence. Plant several varieties along a sidewalk for an easy-to-pick living hedge. As with all espaliered trees, remove wayward branches and maintain the form.

Colonnade apples need little pruning, but you will probably need to remove the occasional branch that is not conforming to the tree's shape.

PESTS AND DISEASES

Apples can live for years and years, but they are prone to a number of pests and diseases. Codling moth is the most common apple pest. The best choices for control are hanging pheromone traps, releasing parasitic wasps, and/or spraying with horticultural oil. Use these controls early enough before infestation gets out of control. Set out traps in the early spring as blossoms appear, and then replace them in about eight weeks. The timing of the release of wasps or spraying depends on your climate; check with local nurseries, the cooperative extension service, or other agricultural agencies in your area for guidelines.

Apple maggots can be a problem, especially in damp areas. You can hang sticky traps, but if they're not effective, you might need to resort to spraying in midsummer. For plum curculio infestations, just after blossom drop in the spring, spread a cloth under the tree, shake all the branches, and then collect the fallen pests and discard them—far away from your garden. Spray trees with a pesticide if this doesn't help.

If leafroller or aphid infestations are small, you can usually let nature take its course; beneficial insects will soon discover

Apple scab is a common disease that requires local knowledge to combat effectively.

and enjoy the banquet that awaits them on the tree. Overwatering can also be the root cause of a pest infestation, so consider less frequent and deeper irrigation cycles.

The most common apple disease is probably apple scab, which leaves hard, crusty spots on the fruit, followed by loss of leaves and small fruit. If you live in an area prone to scab, look for disease-resistant varieties. You can spray for the disease, but it's a complicated process; follow the recommendations for your area for the best results.

Cedar apple rust, powdery mildew, and fireblight also attack apples, especially in cool, damp climates. If these are problems in your area, your first choice for prevention is to plant disease-resistant varieties. Second is to practice good garden maintenance, especially by picking up and discarding fallen fruit and leaves in fall so disease spores cannot overwinter.

Cedar rust can be identified by orange spots that first appear on the leaves as well as spores on lower leaves. Affected

fruit can be small and oddly shaped, dropping before it's ripe. Wind also carries spores from nearby Eastern red cedars, exacerbating the problems for apple trees. In addition to maintaining the growing area, you can also help prevent outbreaks by ensuring that your trees have good air circulation and that soil is in good shape. For more control, use a sulfur spray weekly for about two months, starting when the buds first break.

Powdery mildew can be identified by a whitish powder that appears on leaves. Again, good growing conditions—keeping the tree well and evenly watered and maintaining trees to ensure sunlight and air circulation—can go a long way toward preventing the problem. A strong spray of water when you first notice the infection can help lessen the effect, as can using a fertilizer with a lower nitrogen level. Finally, if the problem is severe, apply a fungicide or a dormant spray after the buds have turned green.

Fireblight is a particular challenge, especially if it gets out of hand. Affected trees have brownish-black leaves and branches that shrivel up and die, making the tree look black and burnt. Fireblight cannot be cured, but you can help prevent the problem by cutting out affected branches well below the disease line (and sterilizing tools between cuts), growing trees in good soil, and not overfertilizing. A dormant spray applied when the buds are green can also help. If you know that fireblight is an issue in your area, select resistant varieties.

Trees can also suffer sunburn. Planting in a location that doesn't get direct and prolonged sunlight will help, as can applying a whitewash (equal parts blend of water and indoor latex paint) or a protective wrap on the trunk.

Early

APPLE VARIETIES

Thousands of apple varieties are available for home gardens, far more than you'll find in even your above-average grocery store or farmers' market. Some of the most popular and best-tasting selections are included here. Some genetic dwarf varieties are also listed, but you'll find standard apples that have been grafted onto dwarfing rootstock to fit small gardens. Be adventurous and try different varieties at apple tastings and grocery stores, and get recommendations for your garden from neighbors and nursery owners.

ANNA

Large, light green fruit with reddish tones. Great for areas with warm winters. Can produce a second crop. Pollinizes 'Dorsett Golden' and 'Ein Shemer'.

BEVERLY HILLS

Small, yellow fruit with touches of red. Tart, but tender. Good for coastal Southern California. Self-pollinating.

CHEHALIS

Large, soft, yellow-green fruit with fairly mild taste. Good for baking. Self-pollinating. Not as susceptible to scab as other apples. Use soon after picking.

Early continued

CORTLAND

Sweet-tart flavor with white flesh that doesn't turn brown after cutting. Self-fruitful. Good fresh, in cooked dishes, or for cider.

DORSETT GOLDEN

Low-chill. Medium, sweet, yellowish fruit. Eat fresh or use for baking and cooking. Pollinizes 'Anna' and 'Ein Shemer'.

EIN SHEMER

Low-chill. Medium-size, yellow fruit. Crisp yet juicy, with a hint of tartness. Pollinizes 'Anna' and 'Dorsett Golden'.

GALA

Medium-size, red and yellow, fragrant fruit. Crisp and juicy. Can bear into midseason. Bears heavily and limbs can break if not supported. Does not store well. Susceptible to fireblight.

GOLDEN RUSSET

Medium yellow to golden fruit with smooth, sweet flesh. Can be used fresh or for cooking. Self-fruitful but a pollinizer produces a better crop.

GRAVENSTEIN

Large, red-striped, crisp, fragrant, juicy fruit. Ideal eaten fresh or cooked. Can bear into midseason. Will not pollinize other apples. Can be susceptible to mildew.

HARALSON

Very hardy. Firm and crisp with a mild flavor. Tree produces abundant fruit that keeps well. Good fresh, baked, or for cider.

HUDSON'S GOLDEN GEM

Hardy. Ripens from early to midseason. Fruit is large and long rather than round; yellow with brownish hue. Nutlike taste makes it a good choice for desserts. Can stay on the tree until winter. Resists fireblight, mildew, and scab.

MOLLIES DELICIOUS

Low-chill. Large, light yellow fruit with tinges of red. Juicy and sweet flesh with great fragrance. Self-fruitful. Stores well.

NORLAND

Hardy Canadian variety. Medium-size, pink fruit with red stripes; not as round as traditional apples. Eat fresh or use in cooked dishes. Stores well.

PINK PEARL

Pale green, medium-size fruit with pink flesh. Very deep pink blossoms. Good mix of sweet and tart flavor. Good for cooking and storing. Needs pollinizer.

Early continued

Midseason

PRISTINE

Medium-size, bright yellow fruit with mild flavor. Use for eating, baking, and sauce. Not as susceptible to fireblight and mildew as some apples; resists scab.

SUMMERRED

Very hardy; not a good choice for areas with hot summers; excellent for colder climates. Medium-size, bright red fruit. Tartness makes it ideal for cooking. Self-fertile.

WILLIAM'S PRIDE

Medium, dark red fruit. Sweet flavor, with a hint of spice, makes it a good choice for eating fresh. Resists scab and cedar rust, with moderate resistance to fireblight and mildew.

ZESTAR!

Cold hardy. Medium-size yellow fruit striped with red. Crispy flesh, juicy, and sweet-tart. Eat fresh or use for baking.

COX'S ORANGE PIPPIN

Medium-size fruit with orange-red skin. Slightly unusual flavor; good for pies, crisps, and other desserts. Does not do well in weather extremes.

DELICIOUS

(*or* 'Red Delicious') Different strains are available; match them to your climate. Look for older varieties for best flavor. Scab can be a problem.

EMPIRE

Somewhat small, dark red fruit with slightly astringent, juicy, crisp flesh. Can be damaged by spring frosts; tolerates hot summers.

FIESTA

Large, dark red fruit with great flavor. Fruit doesn't drop, so thinning is required.

GINGER GOLD

Medium-large, firm and crisp fruit, similar to 'Golden Delicious'. A good early yellow apple. Stores well. Watch for mildew.

GOLDEN DELICIOUS

(*or* 'Yellow Delicious') Medium-large fruit; not related to 'Delicious' ('Red Delicious'). Fragrant, crisp fruit can be eaten fresh or used for cooking. Self-fruitful, but a good pollinizer for other trees.

GORDON

Low-chill and semi-dwarf. Bears for a long time. Fruit is large, tinged with red, and tastes sweet and tart. Needs a pollinizer.

GRANNY SMITH

Late-midseason fruit is yellow-green, firm, and tart. Good cooking choice, but can be eaten fresh. Stores well. Self-fertile.

Midseason continued

HONEYCRISP

Hardy. Medium-size red fruit is crisp, sweet/tart, and great for eating fresh. Resists fireblight, mildew, and scab.

JONAGOLD

Large, red-striped fruit that's firm yet juicy with a slightly tart flavor. Medium-size tree. Won't pollinize other apples; cannot be pollinized by 'Golden Delicious'.

JONATHAN

Small-to-medium, bright red fruit is juicy, tart, and crisp. Good overall apple that keeps well. Can resist scab, but susceptible to mildew. Self-fruitful.

LIBERTY

Hardy. Medium fruit with crisp flesh, ripens late-midseason. Good fresh or cooked. Self-fruitful. Disease resistant.

MCINTOSH

Cool-climate apple with large, bright red fruit and tender white flesh. Strong tart flavor. Subject to scab and excessive fruit drop. Self-fertile.

PETTINGILL

Low-chill. Large, red-on-green apples with firm, tart flesh. Bears into the late season. Large tree. Self-fruitful.

RUBINETTE

Small to medium-size fruit with red stripes. Good for Pacific Northwest and lower Canada. Prized for sweet-tart flavor. Resists mildew and scab.

SPARTAN

Nicely shaped tree with dark red, medium-size, crisp and abundant fruit. Self-fertile.

WEALTHY

(or 'Red Wealthy', 'Double Red Wealthy') Small tree is good for cold areas. Medium to large fruit is firm and tart. Best used for cooking. Good pollinizer.

WINTER BANANA

Low-chill. Large, pale yellow fruit with pink accents. Soft, mild, somewhat bananalike flavor and aroma. Partially self-fruitful and great pollinizer.

WINTER PEARMAIN

(or 'White Winter Pearmain') Low-chill. Pale, medium to large fruit with tender flesh, good flavor.

Late

ARKANSAS BLACK

Medium-size, dark red fruit is firm and crisp. Store for a couple of months and then eat for best flavor. Needs a pollinizer.

ASHMEAD'S KERNAL

Hardy. Small to medium-size fruit is not uniform in shape. Great flavor: crisp, juicy, and sweet. Stores well. Good for dessert, sauce, and cider. Somewhat resistant to mildew and scab.

BRAEBURN

Medium-size, orange-tinged fruit is crisp, with a sweet and tart flavor. Excessive fruit drop in hot climates. Needs thinning otherwise. Mites are a problem.

ENTERPRISE

Sweet, medium-size, firm fruit. Stores well. Resists scab and fireblight, but can drop fruit just before harvest.

FUJI

Relatively low-chill. Medium-size, yellowish fruit with red stripes. Very sweet, firm flesh. Good for storing. Requires a long growing season. Needs pollinizing.

GOLDRUSH

Yellow, medium-size fruit resists mildew and scab and has some fireblight resistance. Tastes best after being stored.

IDARED

Medium to large bright red fruit. Firm flesh sweetens after storage. Heavy producer. Requires pollinizer.

KARMIJN DE SONNAVILLE

Medium-size, yellow fruit with red blush. Great flavor. Can be eaten fresh and keeps well. Sterile; needs pollinizer.

MELROSE

Medium to large, red fruit. Good choice for desserts, with a slightly tart flavor and good aroma. Cross between 'Jonathan' and 'Delicious'. Good pollinizer.

MUTSU

(*or* 'Crispin') Large, tart, crisp green fruit. Great cooking and baking apple, also great out of hand. Large tree needs pollinizer.

NORTHERN SPY

Large, reddish fruit with classic apple taste. Good for cooking and desserts. Keeps well. Also 'Red Spy' and 'Prairie Spy'. Needs pollinizer.

PINK LADY

Moderately low-chill. Medium to large fruit is pink to red over yellow, juicy with a sweet-tart flavor that improves after storage. Can be used fresh or in baking; also good for sauce. Very prone to fireblight. Self-fruitful.

Late <small>continued</small>

Dwarf

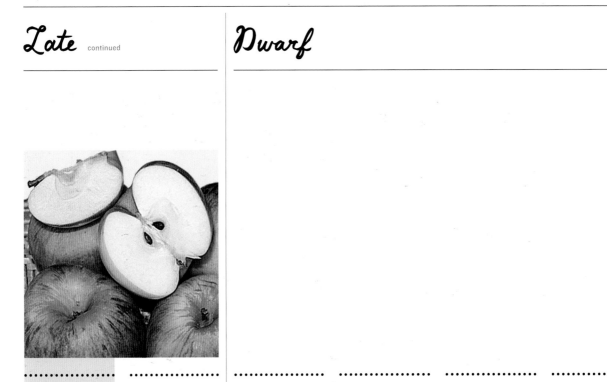

SIERRA BEAUTY

Large, lovely fruit is yellow with red striping. Very firm flesh with sweet-tart flavor. Stores well. Self-fruitful.

SPITZENBERG

(*or* 'Esopus Spitzenberg') Old variety, with medium to large fruit, yellow dotted with red. Tart and spicy. Susceptible to mildew and fireblight. Stores well.

APPLE BABE

Early season dwarf. Pink-red fruit is crisp and sweet.

GARDEN DELICIOUS

Midseason. Genetic dwarf, 8 feet tall and wide at most. Medium-large fruit, golden with hints of red. Self-fertile.

GOLDEN SENTINEL

Midseason. Colonnade. Large, sweet, yellow fruit. Disease resistant. Needs a pollinizer.

SCARLET SENTINEL

Midseason. Colonnade. Prolific producer of large, greenish fruit that is blushed red. Narrow growth to 10 feet. Needs pollinizer. Disease resistant.

Asian pear espalier

Pears

North American gardeners can grow two types of pears. European pears have the traditional pear shape: wider at the bottom than the top. Their flesh is soft and melts in your mouth. Asian pears are round with firm flesh that is crisp and juicy, with just a hint of a gritty texture.

European pears make a statement in the garden. Spring finds the tree covered in white blossoms; come summer, the glossy green leaves brighten the garden, and autumn brings color in shades of gold. Even in winter, the older trees are a treat, with gnarled branches that stand out in a bare garden. Once established, pears are extremely long-lived.

Asian pears were once considered exotic, but these days they're becoming more popular as people have discovered them in grocery stores and farmers' markets. The fruit is extremely fragrant, and as you bite into it, its flavor explodes in your mouth. You might find them labeled as apple pears because of the fruit's resemblance to an apple.

Asian pears can be even more useful as a landscape plant than their European cousins. Standard Asian pear trees reach about two-thirds the size of European trees, but they can be pruned to keep them smaller, making them ideal for home gardens. They tend to grow upright, and their leaves are larger than those of European pears. You'll likely need a second Asian pear for pollination purposes, or planting a grafted tree with more than a single variety will do the trick.

CHOOSING A PEAR: THE BASICS

Your first decision, of course, will be whether you want a European or Asian pear. Both have their plusses and minuses. The decision depends primarily on which fruit appeals to you. If you have room, plant both. Keep in mind that you will have to take responsibility for an extra step in ripening European pears off the tree, while Asian pears can be eaten right away.

When it comes to finding the right European pear variety, temperature, particularly cold, is the most important factor. Because they need a fair amount of winter chill (at least 600 hours), look for a low-chill variety if you live in an area with fairly warm winters. European pears can easily outgrow a small garden, reaching 40 feet tall and 25 feet wide. You can, however, find semi-dwarf varieties or trees that are grafted onto dwarfing rootstock, which keeps them a more manageable size. They're also a good choice to espalier, and dwarf varieties can be grown in large containers.

Asian pears are a good choice for warmer climates, because they don't require as much winter chill (about 400 hours). On the other hand, they can suffer if the temperature drops too low, such as below –15°F. Asian pears can reach up to 30 feet tall and 15 feet wide, but they can be kept to a smaller size by judicious pruning.

Hybrids of European and Asian pears look and taste similar to European pears, but they are slightly smaller and fare better in warmer climates. On the other hand, they bloom earlier than European pears, so late frosts can destroy blossoms and the hope of fruit. Planting in a sheltered spot can help prevent this.

Almost all pears need a second tree for pollination for the best fruit results, although Asian pears can be self-fruitful. Unfortunately for home gardeners, the bloom time for Asian pears is generally earlier than that for European pears, so cross-pollination is not usually an option. Look for multi-grafted rootstocks or convince a neighbor to plant a pear as well.

European pears are notoriously prone to fireblight. If it's a problem in your area, look for a disease-resistant variety. Asian pears are less apt to be affected, but a resistant variety is a good choice for fireblight-plagued regions.

GROWING PEARS

The same growing recommendations apply to all pears, which is another good reason to consider growing both types. As long as the trees will do well in your climate, both can be included in a garden.

GETTING STARTED Choose a European pear or hybrid tree with a strong pyramidal shape and evenly spaced branches. An Asian pear with a strong central leader is the best choice. If you're planning to espalier, choose a tree with strong vertical branching.

Plant bare-root trees in late winter and spring as soon as the soil can be worked. Container-grown trees can be planted throughout the year, but avoid planting in extremely warm or cold weather, even in a mild climate.

As with most fruit trees, pears prefer a sunny spot in well-drained soil. However, like their apple cousins, they will tolerate heavy clay soil and damp roots. Although pears need some winter chill, a spot where cold air pools, such as at the bottom of a hill, can be too cold and can damage the blossoms and limbs. In such cases, place the tree on a slope or higher or against a wall where it can benefit from reflected heat.

Once the pear is place, trim off any errant branches that don't conform to the desired final shape and any branches that look weak or damaged.

GROWING SEASON CARE After you've planted the tree, water it thoroughly. Add mulch, keeping it at least 3 inches away from the trunk, to help keep the soil moist. The soil around the roots should be moist but not soggy. Water deeply and regularly if rainfall is insufficient.

Fertilize in the spring with a balanced fertilizer. Apply about 1 pound of fertilizer per inch of trunk diameter, keeping the fertilizer away from the trunk of the tree. Overfertilizing can lead to excessive leaf growth, which can exacerbate the development of fireblight. If Asian pears show sufficient growth, don't fertilize at all. In general, if a pear tree isn't growing 12 inches or so per season and crops are weak, apply a low-nitrogen fertilizer in the spring before buds open every few years.

You probably won't need to thin European pears or hybrids, but Asian pears are so prolific at setting fruit that you'll likely need to do some fruit thinning. After the fruit has set, thin to one pear per spur, keeping about 6 inches of space between fruits.

HARVESTING Many beginning pear growers wonder why their pears never taste good. The problem is not the pear tree; it's the harvesting method. European pears are tricky. In almost all cases, you pick them before they ripen, when they are still green and hard. One exception is 'Seckel', which can stay on the tree until it's ripe.

To test whether a pear is ready to harvest, check the color. If it is starting to change, gently lift up the fruit. If it's ready, it should snap off the branch. If not, test it again in a few days.

Store European pears until they are ripe. Refrigerate early ripening pears for two to three weeks, and then bring them to room temperature to ripen. Late-ripening pears should be kept in a cool (around 60°F or cooler), dark room; bring them into a warmer room about three days before you plan to eat them so they'll ripen fully. 'Anjou', 'Bosc', and 'Comice' should be kept in a cold spot (at 32°F–40°F) for a month. Then bring them into a warm spot to ripen. Keeping pears slightly underripe and refrigerated is best if you'll be storing them for considerable time.

Fortunately, Asian pears can stay on the tree until they're ripe. Check whether they're ripe as you would for European pears. Unlike many fruits, Asian pears do not ripen all at once, so harvest will extend over a longer period, allowing you time to savor the fruits.

Fireblight damage on the delicious but highly susceptible 'Bartlett' pear

PRUNING

Start pruning young trees at the end of the dormant season. Young trees are vigorous growers, so keep them pruned, especially in a small garden, and encourage a natural yet attractive shape. Both pear types tend to shoot up at first; European pears eventually begin to spread out, while Asian pears remain more upright.

Prune the smaller Asian pears as a central leader. European pears can be pruned to a central leader, but standard and semi-dwarf varieties can grow so tall that reaching the upper fruit can be difficult. Pruning to a modified leader is a better choice.

For all trees, remove branches that are growing from the trunk at a narrow angle. Encourage the branches to spread out by hanging light weights on the limbs, or gently clip a clothespin to the main trunk just above a young shoot, pushing down on the shoot slightly to help increase and encourage a more fruitful branch angle. Larger branches can be trained by placing a stake in the ground, attaching a string from the stake to the branch, and applying gentle tension to pull the branch down.

As trees mature, remove all dead and dying branches as well as any suckers or water sprouts. For older trees, prune to open up the center and to keep the branches from growing too tall. Opening up the center also helps prevent the spread of fireblight by increasing air circulation. Cut back branches with a large number of older fruiting spurs to encourage new growth and avoid overcrowding the fruit. Most pruning should occur in the dormant season, but you can also summer prune to keep the growth of European pears in check.

Pears can also be successfully espaliered. In a small garden, this is a good choice for keeping the trees at a useable size and to keep the fruit easy to reach.

In all cases, it's best to prune consistently. Hard pruning one year can lead to uneven crop production over the next several years.

PESTS AND DISEASES

Fireblight is probably the most troublesome problem for pears, and it can be decidedly serious and quick-moving. The symptoms are obvious. The affected limbs turn black and the leaves look scorched, like a fire has burnt the tree. It kills off branches and distorts the fruit.

Fireblight can be difficult to eradicate. The minute you see affected branches, cut them back well into the area of healthy growth. Err on the side of caution and make the cut 6 to 12 inches from the last visibly infected area. After each cut, disinfect your pruning tools with a 10 percent bleach solution, and then dispose of the infected branches away from your garden. Lush new growth can exacerbate the problem, so fertilize only lightly.

Major pests of the pear include pear psylla and codling moth. Signs of a pear psylla infestation include a blackish mold on stems and leaves that looks similar to fireblight but can be wiped off easily. Keeping the area around the tree free of weeds and debris is the first line of attack. Follow up with a dormant oil spray when the trees are dormant.

Codling moths destroy the fruit; you'll find their caterpillars inside the fruit on the tree or on the ground. To control these pests, first keep the area around the tree weed- and debris-free. In early spring, set out sticky traps. When you see moths in the traps, follow up by releasing parasitic wasps and by wrapping the trunks in a sticky barrier to prevent the caterpillars from reaching the ground, where they overwinter. If the infestation is severe, apply *Bacillus thuringiensis* (Bt) in early spring as well (time its application so it won't harm beneficial insects).

European Pears

PEAR VARIETIES

Your pear choices depend on flavor, harvest season, disease resistance, and storing factors. It also depends on the type of pear you want to grow and the chilling requirements. Far more European pears are available than Asian pears, but you should be able to find some of both for your garden.

ANJOU

(*or* 'd'Anjou', 'Beurre d'Anjou') Round fruit with short neck. Tree grows upright; need to train branches. Ripens late and needs cold storage.

BARTLETT

Medium-large fruit with a long neck and thin skin. Ripens midseason. Usually self-fruitful except in cool climates. Susceptible to fireblight.

BLAKE'S PRIDE

Medium-size yellow-gold fruit with a buttery, rich flavor. Good for eating fresh. Fragrant. Ripens midseason. Highly resistant to fireblight.

European Pears <small>continued</small>

BOSC

(*or* 'Buerre Bosc', 'Golden Russet') Medium-large, long-necked fruit with green or yellow base and brown overtones. Juicy and firm with good flavor. Holds its shape when cooked. Ripens late and needs cold storage. Upright tree needs pruning. Very susceptible to fireblight.

COMICE

(*or* 'Doyenne du Comice', 'Royal Riviera') Large, greenish yellow fruit with brown russeting. Great flavor. Self-fruitful in most areas except in cool climates. Susceptible to fireblight. Late harvest; ripens in cold storage.

CONFERENCE

Large, sweet, juicy pear with buttery flavor. Fruits in clusters. Ripens late. Resistant to fireblight. Needs pollinizer.

FLORDAHOME

Low-chill. Small, light green, juicy fruit ripens early. Resists fireblight. Pollinize with 'Hood'.

HARROW DELIGHT

Hardy. Similar to 'Bartlett' but smaller. Smooth texture. Ripens early. Resists fireblight.

HOOD

Low-chill. Large fruit with yellow-green skin. Strong grower. Ripens early and resists fireblight.

MOONGLOW

Medium-large fruit with short neck is soft and flavorful. Strong grower. Ripens early. Good resistance to fireblight. Needs pollinizer.

ORCAS

Large, with notable pointed stem end. Soft flesh is very flavorful. Ripens midseason. Tree spreads nicely. Moderate fireblight resistance.

RESCUE

Large yellow fruit with red-orange blush. Sweet, juicy flesh; not gritty. Keeps well. Ripens midseason. Self-fertile. Susceptible to fireblight.

European Pears continued

SECKEL

(*or* 'Sugar') Small, sweet, and fragrant. Longtime favorite; good for eating and canning. Does better with a pollinizer, but not 'Bartlett' or any of its strains. Ripens early midseason. Resistant to fireblight.

SUMMER CRISP

Hardy. Small, round pear with crisp and somewhat sweet flesh. Ripens late. Very resistant to fireblight.

SURE CROP

Much like 'Bartlett', but good for areas with late frosts. Ripens late midseason. Resistant to fireblight.

WARREN

Hardy. Medium-large fruit with pale green skin. Buttery flavor. Ripens late. Keeps well. Good resistance to fireblight. Self-fruitful.

WINTER NELIS

Small, round fruit with unattractive skin but a good flavor. Keeps well and good for baking. Ripens late. Somewhat susceptible to fireblight. Does best with pollinizer.

Asian Pears

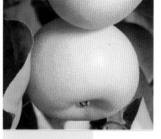

CHOJURO

Russet-green skin. Very strong flavor; might be too tart for some. Good keeper. Ripens late midseason.

HOSUI

Golden brown, very juice, sweet flavor is considered one of the best. Ripens early. Resistant to fireblight.

ICHIBAN

Medium-large, brown fruit with white flesh. Said to taste a bit like butterscotch. Fragile skin. Ripens early.

KIKUSUI

Medium-size, somewhat flat, yellow-green fruit is sweet and juicy. Good for eating fresh. Ripens midseason. Resistant to fireblight.

KOREAN GIANT

Hardy. Extremely large olive-green fruit can weigh a pound or more. Juicy and sweet. Ripens late. Keeps well in cold storage.

Asian Pears continued

KOSUI

Strong-growing tree with small, yellow-brown, sweet and crisp fruit. Ripens early. Can be stored.

NIJISSEIKI

(*or* 'Twentieth Century') Cold hardy. Medium-size, oddly shaped fruit with yellow skin. Juicy and crisp, mild flavor. Tolerates drought but is not disease-resistant.

SEURI

Large orange-tinged fruit with a good fragrance. Ripens late, but not a good keeper.

SHINKO

Brownish fruit with juicy, sweet, crisp flesh; good flavor. Ripens late and stores well.

SHINSEIKI

Medium to large, yellow fruit with mildly sweet flavor. Ripens early and stores well. Resists disease. Self-fruitful.

Hybrid Pears

SHINSUI

Small to medium, very sweet, crunchy fruit with yellow-brown skin. Ripens early.

YA LI

Low-chill. An old variety with green, traditional pear-shaped fruit, sweet taste. Great fall foliage. Ripens late, stores well. Resistant to fireblight.

FAN-STIL

Low-chill. Medium-size yellow fruit. Crisp and juicy. Eat fresh or use cooked. Ripens midseason. Good resistance to fireblight.

KIEFFER

Low-chill. Medium-large, oval-shaped fruit is best for canning and baking. Ripens late. Good resistance to fireblight. Self-fruitful.

ORIENT

Large fruit, yellow with russeting. Juicy and firm; not as sweet as some pears. Use for canning and baking. Ripens late. Very good resistance to fireblight. Needs pollinizer.

URE

Hardy. Small fruit is sweet and juicy; eat fresh or can. Ripens midseason. Good resistance to fireblight.

The quince is delicious reminder that fall is on its way.

Quinces

Although the flowering quince (*Chaenomeles species*) is better known to many gardeners, the fruiting quince (*Cydonia oblonga*) is a versatile and surprisingly hardy landscape plant with spring flowers, fall fruit, and lovely twisted branches that create a beautiful focal point in the winter garden.

Quince is a slow-growing tree or shrub, reaching 10 to 25 feet tall and wide. After it has matured, a quince will live a long time. Spring brings large white or pale pink flowers that resemble wild roses. In summer, the dark green leaves with white underbellies create a backdrop for other brightly colored plants. The tree doesn't disappoint in the fall: the round or pear-shaped, somewhat fuzzy, yellow-skinned fruit is complemented by the yellow autumn leaves.

The fruit's taste is reminiscent of apple, but it is not usually considered a "pick off the tree and eat" fruit, since most varieties are tart and somewhat dry. Instead, quince is a great choice for jams, jellies, and preserves. Its tartness adds a piquant flavor in pies when mixed with other fruits, especially apples, and it can be used to make candy. Some quince varieties are sweet enough to eat fresh.

CHOOSING A QUINCE: THE BASICS

Your main priorities in choosing a quince are a strong tree with evenly spaced branches. A few quince varieties are available. If you taste one and like it, look for that variety. For very small gardens, smaller varieties can be planted in a half barrel or other large container. Quince is also a great candidate for traditional espalier training. Quinces are self-fertile.

GROWING QUINCES

Quinces are surprisingly easy to grow. Your main jobs will be watering, fertilizing, some light pruning, and keeping fireblight under control. Even these chores are relatively light compared to those required for other fruit trees.

GETTING STARTED Bare-root trees can be planted in late winter or early spring; container-grown trees can be planted any time from early fall to early summer (before it gets too hot). Look for a sunny spot with good drainage. Don't plant the tree too deeply; keep the soil line on the trunk of container-grown trees even or slightly above the planted soil line and keep bare-root trees at about that same depth. Quinces can grow in almost all soils.

After the tree is in the ground, water it deeply and add mulch from about 3 inches out from the base of the trunk to the drip line. Remove any weak or wayward branches at this time.

GROWING SEASON CARE A quince is a low-maintenance plant. Water and fertilizer are the main requirements during the growing season. Water deeply on a two- or three-week schedule. Apply a light helping of a low-nitrogen fertilizer across the root zone in late winter and again in early summer. Quinces don't need to be thinned unless heavy fruit threatens to break the branches. Stakes can be used to help support heavily laden branches.

HARVESTING Harvest fruit in the fall after it is fully yellow, with no green showing. When its color and rich fragrance tells you it is ripe; twist the fruit away from the stem. Although the fruit looks sturdy, it can bruise easily, so be gentle when handling it.

After harvest, you can store quince for a couple of months in the refrigerator.

PRUNING

A quince grows naturally as a shrub, but it can be pruned to a tree form. To maintain the shrub form, leave up to five main central branches and remove side branches to keep the shrub to an open form. For a tree, remove multiple central stems in late winter to a single central trunk, and then prune branches to encourage a modified central leader form. Keeping the center of the tree open helps with air circulation and helps prevent the development of fireblight. Throughout the first few years, cut back the branches by about half to keep the plant in bounds. After that, prune to shape and remove any dead, weak, or crossing branches. Remove any suckers at the base of the tree at any time.

PESTS AND DISEASES

Fireblight is the only disease you'll probably encounter with a quince, but that can be very serious. As its name implies, this disease mimics the look of a tree that has been scorched by fire, with brown curled leaves and blackened branches. It spreads easily and can be difficult to eradicate after it has gained a foothold.

The first and best approach is prevention. Keep the tree well-watered, but avoid overwatering and soggy roots. Do not add fertilizer with too much nitrogen, which will stimulate excessive growth. Keep the tree or shrub pruned and relatively open so air can circulate freely.

If your quince is attacked by fireblight, prune off affected branches 6 to 12 inches below where the disease appears. Sterilize your pruning tools between cuts and after you've finished, and dispose of the affected branches away from your garden.

You might also have problems with codling moths, but large infestations are unusual. Codling moth larvae are found inside the fruit. To keep the insects in check, keep the ground around the plant free of debris and weeds. If moths continue to be a problem, hang pheromone traps or sticky traps. Releasing parasitic wasps or spraying with *Bacillus thuringiensis* (Bt) before the larvae enter the fruit can also help.

Quinces

QUINCE VARIETIES

Although far fewer varieties of quince are available than apple or pear varieties, you'll find plenty from which to choose, from apple- or pear-shaped varieties, to tangy or sweet-flavored selections.

AROMATNAYA

Medium-sized, apple-shaped fruit with yellow flesh and a pineapple flavor. One of the few quinces that can be eaten fresh. Soften at room temperature before eating.

CHAMPION

Hardy quince with yellow, very sweet fruit; can be eaten fresh. Late season.

COOKE'S JUMBO

Pear-shaped fruit with white flesh. One of the largest quinces, close to double the size of others; single fruit can weigh more than a pound.

HAVRAN

Large, pear-shaped fruit with very sweet white flesh.

ORANGE

(*or* 'Apple') An older variety. Fruit is apple-shaped, and the flesh is orangish in color. Ripens early.

PINEAPPLE

Developed by Luther Burbank. Good for cooking or eating fresh. Has a pineapple-like flavor when cooked. Allow time to ripen fully on the tree.

PORTUGAL

Pear-shaped fruit that turns pinkish-red when cooked. Ripens early. Prefers a pollinizer.

SMYRNA

Fragrant, round, bright yellow fruit with white flesh. Great for cooking.

VAN DEMAN

Developed by Luther Burbank. Large, oblong shaped, spicy tasting fruit with yellow flesh.

Citrus

As a gardener, if you live in citrus-growing territory, you're in luck. Citrus are one of the most easily grown fruit trees. They are generally free of fuss and problems, and their evergreen nature, fragrant white flowers, and long-lasting fruit makes them a

A small sampling of the citrus fruits available for you to grow and enjoy

standout in any garden. Their fruit is also welcome as a staple in every meal, from breakfast to dinner, including some outstanding desserts. Lemon meringue pie, anyone?

Unfortunately, the citrus-growing region is fairly limited in North America. The best growing areas are in Florida, along the Gulf Coast, and from the lower Arizona desert northwest to northern California. A more marginal area extends from the southern tip of South Carolina to lower Texas and from Arizona up through the central valley of California to the Pacific Northwest coast. Elsewhere, citrus can be grown in containers that can be moved indoors to a cool area with bright light for the colder months.

CHOOSING A CITRUS: THE BASICS

Citrus choices are plentiful. Although oranges and lemons often come to mind when you think of citrus, consider expanding beyond that to mandarin oranges, limes, grapefruits, and kumquats. Hybrids are expanding the available options as well, or try some of the more exotic options such as citron and pummelo. If you can't decide, try planting more than one citrus in a single hole, or look for a tree with several different citrus grafted onto a single trunk. (The only caveat here is that you'll need to keep the more vigorous growers in check with heavier pruning to allow the other grafted varieties to gain a foothold. Fortunately, citrus handle pruning, even heavy pruning, with ease, and most are happy with the same general climate conditions and seasonal care.)

There is hope for gardeners in areas not considered suitable for growing citrus. Your climate might not be hospitable to citrus planted in the ground, but the trees make great container plants. They can be moved indoors to a cool area with bright light for the colder months, and you can carry them outside in summer to benefit from the warmth and sunshine. Some favorites, such as 'Improved Meyer' lemon, 'Bearss' lime, 'Calamondin' mandarin, and kumquats, are likely to produce fruit even if they're grown inside as houseplants—but even if they don't produce fruit, these beautiful evergreen plants will brighten any indoor space.

A potted 'Moro' blood orange ripens fruit more consistently than the same variety planted in the soil nearby because of the radiant heat reflected from the pot and patio.

GROWING CITRUS

Most citrus are sold in containers. Look for a well-shaped plant with healthy leaves, no sign of pests or damage on the branches, and a strong central trunk. Citrus can also be espaliered; choose a tree whose form generally follows the eventual shape you want to achieve.

GETTING STARTED Plant citrus in full sun, where it will be sheltered from cold winds and cold spots. The trees require well-drained, well-aerated soil so the roots don't become waterlogged. If soil drainage is insufficient, plant citrus in a raised bed or on a rise of soil, and add plenty of organic matter before planting, although that won't completely compensate for poor-draining soil.

Trees can be planted year-round, but do not plant during weather extremes to avoid stressing the tree. If you plant in fall, wait until spring to prune it.

Create a moatlike watering basin around the tree that starts about 12 inches from the trunk of the tree and extends past the spread of the branches—citrus roots spread widely and deeply. Water deeply after planting, and remove any fruit currently on the tree.

If you're planting in a container, use a light and well-drained soil mix. For best results, look for a relatively large container and make the plant a focal point.

After the tree is planted, add a 2–3 inch layer of mulch to help retain moisture; keep mulch about 3 inches away from the trunk or stem. If you live in a marginal area for citrus, add pebbles or gravel as a mulch; the stones will help reflect heat onto the tree.

GROWING SEASON CARE Water citrus consistently to prevent the fruit from splitting, but don't let the roots get waterlogged. After the plants are established, they can handle being watered every other week during the summer. Water deeply; for most soils, this means running a drip system for a few hours to reach the deepest roots, which can be 4 feet below the surface.

Even with the best of soil, citrus will need regular applications of nutrients, particularly nitrogen. A citrus fertilizer is always a good choice. When you plant the tree, apply about 2 ounces of actual nitrogen (check the label to determine how much fertilizer you should apply to reach that amount). Increase it by 4 ounces per year for the next four years. After that, apply about 1 to 1½ pounds actual nitrogen early (cut this amount by up to a half for trees in containers). Apply phosphorus and potassium as well, although in lesser amounts.

Don't apply too much fertilizer all at once. If freezes are likely, feed plants in late winter through summer, after watering thoroughly. Otherwise, feed regularly throughout the year, especially if your trees are planted in sandy soil or you get

A stone planter holds and reflects heat, which can help extend the growing range of citrus.

ROOT PRUNING

If a tree's roots are taking up most of the (or the entire) pot, leaving no room for soil, nutrients, and water, and you don't want to transplant to a larger container, you can root-prune to remove some of the roots. This might seem like a drastic measure, but a healthy tree can handle it, and root pruning will often help rejuvenate the plant. You might need to do this every few years for container-bound plants.

In spring or early fall, remove the plant from the container; letting the soil dry out for a few days beforehand will make this easier. Gently untangle the roots and spread them out, removing as much soil as possible. Using a saw, cut back the large and medium-size roots by up to a third (you might want to do this gradually over two or three years rather than all at once). If the tree is severely root-bound, remove any encircling roots and cut three wedge-shaped slices into the sides of the root ball (you'll be cutting through a few tangled roots) using a very sharp knife or blade. Clean the container and add fresh amended soil, and then repot the tree. Water thoroughly, and keep the tree in a sheltered and shaded spot for the next couple of weeks to allow it time to adjust.

a lot of rain, which can wash nutrients out of the soil. Keep the fertilizer away from the trunk of the tree, and water deeply after applying.

Other than feeding and watering, citrus are fairly low-maintenance plants. Keep the area around the tree free of weeds and clean up debris, such as fallen fruits. Although you might need to deal with some pest problems such as aphids and scale, citrus don't require regular spraying.

HARVESTING Do not pick citrus before the fruit is ripe; the fruit ripens only on the tree. The good news is that unless you are expecting a hard freeze, most citrus can stay on the tree for some time. The best way to determine whether citrus is ripe is by taste; skin color is not necessarily a good indication. Twist the fruit as you pull it from the tree, or use clippers to cut off fruit at the stem. This latter method is the only way you should harvest mandarin oranges; their loose skin will tear if you twist them from the tree.

PRUNING

Prune to remove unwanted branches and make the tree look aesthetically pleasing. You can prune citrus trees at any time, but spring is best. Remove suckers and water sprouts; dead, diseased, and broken branches; and any branches that are not producing fruit. Also remove branches that are growing too tall or that don't conform to the desired shape.

Citrus are forgiving and can be pruned to almost any shape. For a tree, remove lower branches to train the plant to a central trunk with a rounded top. For a shrub, retain multiple trunks and shape the tree to the preferred form, be that rounded or upright. For an espalier, follow the general guidelines to attain the shape you want. Be aware that although an espalier is ideal for a small space, it might produce less fruit than a standard tree. Sour oranges, in particular, can be grown as a hedge.

PESTS AND DISEASES

Most citrus are not trouble-prone. For the most part, citrus will thrive without the attention other fruit trees require. Nitrogen deficiency is the most likely problem you'll have to address. Leaf color is the first indication of nitrogen problems: heavy growth and dark green foliage that looks burned at the edges means the tree is getting too much nitrogen; too little nitrogen, and the leaves turn yellow.

Yellow leaves can also indicate chlorosis (the general term for a lack of iron, zinc, or manganese) or overwatering. If a tree is low in iron, the leaves turn yellow, starting at the edges, and the veins remain green (this could also indicate too much water, so check that first). Mottled leaves generally indicate manganese deficiency, and yellow blotches or mottling indicate a lack of zinc. These symptoms can be difficult to differentiate; to cover all your bases, look for a product containing manganese, iron, and zinc chelates to address the problem. Winter chlorosis is common in the cool season when soil nutrients are less available. Healthy trees will spring back as the weather warms.

Insects such as aphids, leaf miners, mealybugs, scale, and whiteflies can be problematic, but in most cases natural predators will appear and eliminate the pest before you need to take steps. Should an infestation continue, use a blast of water to remove the insects from the tree, or use a spray of water with a bit of dishwashing liquid (one that's environmentally friendly and not antibacterial) or a safe insecticide. If problems with leaf miners and scale continue, use horticultural oil in early spring.

Snails and slugs can also cause problems for citrus. If the infestation is small, hand pick and destroy them in the evenings or early mornings when they are active. For serious problems, try snail repellents that are not harmful to the environment, or place copper bands around the base of the tree; copper repels snails and slugs. Keep the area around the trees free of debris, shrubs, and plants that can provide hiding places. Be vigilant: gastropods are remarkably effective at munching their way through our gardens.

Citrus bud mites can appear on citrus in some areas. These tiny insects are difficult to see, but the deformed fruit will give them away. To check for these insects, put a sheet of white paper under a deformed fruit, gently tap the tree, and look for tiny red, yellow, or green specks scurrying across the paper. To control, spray with horticultural oil in spring and fall.

Citrus are fairly disease-resistant. Root rot and fungal problems are most likely the result of poor drainage; change your watering schedule to allow the soil time to dry out between waterings. Occasionally older trees will develop brown rot gummosis. Cleaning wounds, removing decayed bark, and keeping the base of the trunk dry will help lessen the problem. You can also paint the areas with a paste of Bordeaux mixture (a mixture of copper sulfate and hydrated lime used as a fungicide). If a plant develops the greasy spot fungus, indicated by yellow and brown spots on the leaves' undersides, apply a copper fungicide or horticultural oil.

In Florida, citrus canker can be a problem. It can be identified by deep brown spots ringed with yellow that appear on the fruit. No real controls exist, but local nurseries or cooperative extension offices can advise you about suggested remedies in your area.

CULTURAL PROBLEMS

Citrus are susceptible to sunburn in summer and extended periods below freezing in winter. Sunburn usually affects newly planted trees in particularly sunny areas. Wrap trunks in special tree wraps designed for this purpose. Limbs that are newly exposed after pruning can also be affected; paint whitewash or a 50/50 latex paint/water (not exterior paint) mixture on the branches to protect them.

If a freeze is expected, protect smaller trees and shrubs by placing a lightweight tent of cloth or plastic over them, taking care not to let the tent walls touch the leaves. Try stringing old-fashioned Christmas-tree lights (not the newer LED lights) through the branches of both small and large citrus bushes and trees and turn these on at night. The warmth from the bulbs will help protect the plants from freezing.

Oranges

The sweet orange is the king of the citrus family. They can be pruned as trees or as large shrubs, and their glossy foliage makes them a great landscape plant throughout the year. Although the trees can grow fairly large, you can easily prune them to keep fruits within picking range. Dwarf varieties of your favorite sweet oranges can be planted in pots to enliven a patio or porch and keep fruit within easy reach.

Most oranges bear fruit in fall and winter, but Valencia oranges bear fruit from late winter to early summer. The good news is that unless you are expecting freezing weather, oranges can stay on the tree for months, and cool weather will actually help the sugars develop, making them taste sweeter.

CHOOSING AN ORANGE: THE BASICS

When it comes to deciding what orange to grow, your most important consideration is the climate in your garden. Not only do sweet oranges require a certain amount of heat to produce tasty fruit, but they also have varying levels of frost tolerance. They can take some frosty days, but too much cold can result in permanent damage. In areas where freezing is likely, look for cold-tolerant varieties.

The two most popular oranges are navel oranges, of which 'Washington' is the most widely planted, and Valencia types, which are the most widely planted of all the oranges and the source of the orange juice sold in grocery stores. The type you choose depends on where you garden.

Navel oranges need a fair amount of heat. The fruit ripens fairly quickly in the fall, and trees can continue to produce fruit into the winter if they have sufficient summer heat. Standard navel oranges grow on medium-size trees of 20 to 25 feet tall with a rounded shape.

Valencia oranges don't need as much heat as navel oranges and are more frost-tolerant. They are a good choice for Southern California and other warm climates, but they don't thrive in desert environments. The standard trees are larger than the navels and grow vigorously. Unlike navels, Valencia

oranges ripen from late winter to early summer, and they benefit from remaining on the tree because they get sweeter the longer they hang.

Other sweet orange varieties don't fall into either of these categories, such as Arizona Sweets, which grow well in desert gardens and produce fruit in the fall. The trees are generally large, although a semi-dwarf variety is available.

Blood oranges are highly distinctive, with red flesh, juice, and rinds. After you get over the color, you'll find these smallish fruits generally sweet and juicy, with an interesting berry undertone. They thrive where other sweet oranges thrive. The depth of color varies depending on the variety. Blood orange trees are not overly large, at 10 to 20 feet tall, with a canopy that is round and tends to spread. The fragrant and glossy leaves attract both birds and butterflies, and blossoms cover the tree in spring.

Although sour oranges produce fairly bitter fruit, their huge, perfumed flowers and long, dark leaves make them a landscape standout. The trees range in size from small (10 feet or shorter) to fairly large (up to 30 feet) and tend to grow more upright than sweet oranges. The dark orange-red fruit ripens from fall to winter, but it can stay on the tree for up to a year. Sour oranges are not good for eating out of hand, but they can be used for an excellent marmalade. They're also more cold-tolerant than their sweet cousins.

Navel Oranges

ORANGE VARIETIES

Most popular orange varieties, especially navel oranges, are also available on dwarfing rootstock if you want a smaller plant. Check carefully to determine the plant's final size, because many varieties sold as dwarf trees are grafted onto rootstock that is more semi-dwarf, and the trees can reach up to 15 feet tall.

CARA CARA

Large fruit with unusual pink to red flesh (depending on where it's grown). Strong and sweet orange flavor. Bears fruit from autumn through midwinter.

LANE LATE

Ripens from late winter into early summer. Good flavor for eating or juicing.

ROBERTSON

Early ripening fruit looks and tastes similar to 'Washington' oranges. Abundant fruit grows in clusters on dwarf tree, to 8 feet.

Valencia Oranges

SKAGGS BONANZA

Early ripener. Small tree produces lots of fruit. Fruit does not age well if it remains on the tree.

WASHINGTON

Original and most popular navel orange with great flavor. Thrives in warmer inland climates, but underperforms in desert areas. Standard tree reaches 20–25 feet; dwarf stock grows up to 12 feet. Bears fruit from fall through the midwinter. Fruit can stay on the tree for up to four months.

CAMPBELL

Juice orange. Ripens earlier than 'Valencia', with almost no seeds.

DELTA

Juice orange, similar to 'Valencia', but ripens earlier, with almost no seeds. Fruit tends to grow within the canopy, which helps protect it from frost damage.

MIDKNIGHT

Ripens earlier than 'Valencia'. Great flavor and a few seeds.

Valencia Oranges continued

Other Sweet Oranges

VALENCIA

Classic juice orange. Medium to large fruit is more tart than navel oranges. Ripens from late winter to early summer. Fruit can stay on the tree for months and keeps growing. Crops alternate from heavy to light. One of the largest orange trees; even dwarf varieties tend to be larger than navel orange trees.

DILLER

Arizona Sweet. Ideal for desert climate. Large tree with large leaves; smaller fruit size than other oranges. Fruit is seedless and ripens in the late fall; ideal for juice. The tree can handle frost.

HAMLIN

Arizona Sweet. Large tree, similar to 'Diller' with small to medium-size, juicy fruit. Not as cold hardy as other Arizona Sweets.

MARRS

Arizona Sweet. Naturally semi-dwarf tree bears early-ripening fruit at a young age. Good eating orange.

PARSON BROWN

Early-season juice orange with small, seedy fruit. A favorite in Florida gardens.

PINEAPPLE

Arizona Sweet. Midseason juice orange. Not as cold hardy as other Arizona Sweets. Medium-size, seedy fruit with rich flavor. Tree will drop fruit.

SHAMOUTI

(*or* 'Jaffa', 'Palestine Jaffa') Large, seedless fruit with a thick skin; good for eating. Dwarf varieties are common, with beautiful form and foliage; tend to be wider than tall. Bears fruit in early spring.

TROVITA

Nice flavor. Good for cooler climates, but tolerates desert heat. Dwarf variety has beautiful, dark green leaves. Ripens in early spring.

Blood Oranges

MORO

Distinctive fruit with deep red flesh. Rind color from orange to red, depending on climate. Rich sweet-tart flavor. One of the few blood oranges that thrives in coastal Northern California.

SANGUINELLI

Red rind and flesh on small, spicy, sweet-tart, oval fruit from late winter to midspring. Good container choice.

TAROCCO

Reddish or pinkish fruit in early and midwinter. Color can vary. Good for colder areas. More open growing than most oranges. Standards are the largest of the blood oranges; dwarf varieties are a good for espalier.

Sour Oranges

BOUQUET DE FLEURS

(*or* 'Bouquet') Best grown as a shrub or small tree; 8 to 10 feet. Thornless branches, with dark green foliage. Large flowers are extremely fragrant. Bitter and almost seedless fruit. Makes a good hedge.

CHINOTTO

(*or* myrtle leaf orange) Very dense plant with small leaves, reaches 7 to 20 feet, but grows slowly. Can be grown in a tub or container. Easy to shape. Fruit is small and bright, unsuitable for eating fresh but good candied.

SEVILLE

The classic sour orange. Standout ornamental tree or hedge plant, to 20 feet. Seedy fruit makes wonderful marmalade.

Mandarins

Mandarin and mandarin hybrids are plentiful, and more varieties are introduced each year. They are also sold as tangerines, satsumas, clementines, tangelos, tangors, and sour-acid mandarins, and by specific names such as 'Pixie' and 'Delight'. These are all a type of mandarin orange or a mandarin hybrid.

Mandarin hybrids include straight crosses between mandarins and another citrus as well as complex combinations. Both tangelos, which are crosses between mandarins and grapefruits, and tangors, a mandarin and orange cross, are among the many hybrids. Sour-acid mandarin fruit (such as 'Calamondin' and 'Rangpur') can be used for marmalades and as a base for drinks, but their flesh is usually too sour to eat fresh.

CHOOSING A MANDARIN
As with other citrus, mandarins and mandarin hybrids are evergreen and easy to grow if you live in the appropriate climate. Pests and diseases are few and far between. Pruning is needed simply to shape the plant as either a tree or a shrub and to remove wayward, broken, or diseased branches.

Mandarins

MANDARIN VARIETIES

Armed with information such as whether the variety is a true mandarin or a hybrid, general tree size, fruit color and size, and general seediness, you should be able to make an informed decision about which is the right mandarin for your garden.

CALAMONDIN

Sour-acid mandarin variety; cross of mandarin and kumquat. Upright form; 7 to 15 feet tall. Fruit is generally small and yellow or yellow-orange. Sweet edible rind; flesh is juicy but sour. Bears throughout the year and fruit stays on the tree. Can be grown indoors.

CLEMENTINE

Small tree with attractive weeping form and lots of foliage; dwarf form is ideal for containers and small spaces. Early fruit is reddish orange and very sweet, though often seedy, with a strong fragrance. Best with pollinizer. Once ripe, fruit quality will not degrade much if it remains on the tree.

DANCY

This tangerine often appears in Christmas stockings. Small fruit usually has lots of seeds and strong flavor. Ripens late fall through winter. Large tree with an upright form. Dwarf form is good for containers or espalier.

ENCORE

Medium-size upright tree with dense foliage and slim, spreading branches. Yellow to deep-orange fruit is seedy and tart, but juicy. Fruit ripens in summer and can remain on the tree until fall.

FAIRCHILD

Hybrid of 'Clementine' and 'Orlando' tangelo. Medium-size, spreading tree with few thorns. Needs heat to produce good fruit. Good for desert areas. Medium-size, early to midseason fruit is sweet and juicy, with dark reddish orange skin that's easy to peel; tends to be seedy. Best with pollinizer.

FREMONT

Moderate, almost thornless tree with upright form. Medium-size, sweet-tart, seedy fruit with good flavor; ripens fall to winter. Can bear alternately heavy, and then light crops. Thin fruit if necessary. Prone to sunburn.

GOLD NUGGET

Medium-size tree with upright form. Seedless fruit with a light, bright rind that is easy to peel. Sweet, strong flavor. Ripens in the late winter to spring and will hold on the tree.

HONEY

Tree can be large and spreading, with small, sweet fruit. Ripens early but will hold on the tree. Not the same as the honey tangerines sold in markets, which is usually 'Murcott'.

Mandarins continued

KARA

Thornless tree, to 20 feet tall, with weeping branches and large leaves. Large fruit will not sweeten until it is very ripe. Ripens late, and can hold on the tree. A dwarf form, half the size of a standard, is available.

KINNOW

Attractive, symmetrical, upright tree with long, thin branches. Can reach 20 feet; dwarf form to about 10 feet. Good choice for most citrus-friendly climates. Fruit is medium-size, with a rich flavor, good aroma, and lots of seeds. Ripens from winter to early spring, but will hold on the tree.

MEDITERRANEAN

(*or* 'Willow Leaf') Medium-size, spreading tree with willowlike branches and narrow leaves; the mandarin of the Mediterranean. Needs heat to produce well. Light-orange fruit ripens midseason and is mildly sweet, juicy, and aromatic. Pick when ripe; does not keep well.

MINNEOLA

Tangelo. Vigorously growing large tree with large pointed leaves. Fruit is deep reddish orange; flesh is orange with a tart but rich taste and few seeds. Ripens midseason to late. Best with pollinizer, although 'Orlando' is not a good choice.

MURCOTT

(*or* 'Murcott Honey', sometimes sold as honey tangerine) Tangor. Upright tree does not thrive in cold weather. Medium-size fruit has a thin rind that is difficult to peel. Fruit is juicy and rich; can be seedy. Ripens late and does not store well.

NOVA

Hybrid. Larger tree that tends to be thorny. Sweet, juicy fruit. Often sold as a tangelo. Ripens early to midseason. Needs pollinizer.

ORLANDO

Tangelo. Medium-size to large tree with cupped leaves; fairly cold tolerant. Medium to large fruit has orange skin and flesh and is juicy and somewhat sweet. Ripens very early and will not hold on the tree. Best with pollinizer, but not 'Minneola'.

ORTANIQUE

Tangor. Medium-size to large tree bears fruit late in the season. Fruit has bright orange peel and is fragrant, sweet, and juicy. Generally seedy. Ripens late and holds well on the tree. Good choice for marmalade.

PAGE

Clementine and tangelo hybrid. Medium to large tree is a good landscape choice with plenty of foliage, rounded shape, and almost no thorns. Fruit is small and extremely tasty and sweet, good for both eating fresh and juice. Ripens early. Will hold on the tree.

PIXIE

Large, upright tree thrives in mild climates. Light orange, smallish fruit is seedless, juicy, and sweet. Yellow-orange skin is somewhat rough but peels easily. Ripens midseason to late.

RANGPUR

(or 'Rangpur' lime) Sour-acid variety. Medium-size tree with a spreading and weeping habit. Tolerates cold. Fruit resembles a mandarin and is acidic but not as tart as a lime. Good as a base for drinks and dressings. Bears fruit throughout the year and holds well on the tree.

Mandarins continued

ROBINSON

Hybrid. Large, upright tree is also available as a dwarf. Cold hardy. Medium-size, deep orange fruit is very sweet. Ripens early and tends to split. Seedy, especially with pollination.

SATSUMA

Several varieties are sold as satsuma. These are the canned mandarins on grocery shelves. Trees reach up to 15 feet and are more open and spreading than most mandarins. Dwarf trees, to 6 feet, can be trained as shrubs.

More cold hardy than other mandarins. Fruit is large with a sweet, light flavor and loose skin. Ripens early and needs to be picked when ripe, but can be stored after harvest.

SEEDLESS KISHU

Small to medium-size tree with small, seedless, flavorful fruit that's easy to peel. Great for eating fresh. Ripens early and will hold for a while on the tree.

SUNBURST

Medium to large tree with large, reddish orange fruit early in the season. Mild, sweet flavor. Without a pollinizer it has almost no seeds.

W. MURCOTT

Fruit often sold as 'Delite'. Medium-size tree. Midseason to late fruit with bright orange peel and great flavor. If pollinated, will become seedy. Fruit keeps well on the tree. 'Tango' is the seedless form.

'Meyer' lemons show the orange in their parentage in their flavor and color as they ripen.

Lemons

If oranges are the kings of the citrus, lemons are the queens. As a culinary superstar, they are prized around the world for their flavor and fragrance. All parts of the lemon can be used, from the peel, to the rind, to the flesh. They are used in preserves, added for flavor to main courses, included in baked items, and used as a garnish. And where would we be without lemonade in the summer?

Lemon trees can grow throughout a larger geographic area than oranges. They are vigorous growers that reach 20 to 25 feet tall, although trees on dwarfing rootstocks are readily available. Still, even a standard tree is a great choice for a small garden. Lemon trees actually profit from being pruned back regularly, and the light green leaves and fragrant white blossoms that bloom year-round in some climates are impressive.

Most ripe lemons can remain on the tree for some time, but some, such as 'Lisbon', need to be picked as soon as they ripen. In any event, don't allow lemons to remain on the tree too long or the flavor and quality of the flesh will decline. If stressed for water, the tree can draw moisture out of the fruit. Taste the fruit often to determine when it is at its peak.

CHOOSING A LEMON: THE BASICS

Lemons don't require as much heat as oranges, and this increases your options if you garden in marginal areas. Your main concern will be the tree's cold tolerance.

Lemons

LEMON VARIETIES

Most lemon varieties are available as either standard or dwarf forms. If you're looking for a dwarf tree, check before you buy to find out just how big it will grow. Some selections sold as dwarf trees are actually semi-dwarf plants that can outgrow small spaces or containers.

BEARSS

Classic lemon (unrelated to the 'Bearss' lime) in looks and flavor. A fast grower with lots of thorns, it's grown primarily in Florida. Bears fruit year-round, but crops are heavier in fall and winter.

EUREKA

A true classic lemon. Trees, to 20 feet, are fairly open with relatively few thorns. Dwarf varieties, to 10 feet, are denser. New leaves are almost purple, becoming dark green at maturity. Bears fruit year-round, but not usually overly prolific at any one time. Skin is fairly thin; fruit is juicy and acidic with few seeds. A good choice for espalier.

IMPROVED MEYER

A disease-free form and the only 'Meyer' lemon that can be sold in California. Fruit is rounder and darker yellow than 'Eureka'. Sweeter and juicier than other lemons. Starts bearing fruit year-round at an early age. Standard trees can be 12 feet tall and 15 feet wide, but those on dwarf rootstocks are half that size. Good choice for containers.

LISBON

Upright tree with lots of thorns; to 25 feet. Usually a shrub but can be trained as a small tree. Prune regularly to keep size in check. Fruit tastes similar to 'Eureka' and ripens year-round, with heaviest crop in fall. Somewhat more cold and heat resistant than 'Eureka'. Look for a seedless form. Pick fruit when it ripens.

PONDEROSA

Very thorny tree, to 10 feet for a standard, 6 feet for a dwarf. Large fruit with a mild taste and thick rind. Most fruit ripens in winter, but some ripens year-round. Frost sensitive. Dwarf variety good for espalier.

Lemons continued

SUNGOLD

Semi-dwarf variety, to 14 feet and half again as wide. Fruit is yellow with green stripes; leaves are green with mottled white. Ripens in fall and winter.

VARIEGATED PINK EUREKA

(*or* 'Pink Lemonade') 'Eureka' sport. Variegated green-and-white leaves with a purplish tinge stand out in the landscape. Fruit is also variegated before it ripens. Good choice for containers; stays under 8 feet. Fruit not as tasty as other lemons, but juicy. Frost sensitive.

VILLA FRANCA

Large, dense, fast-grower. Tree and fruit resemble 'Eureka'. Ripens fall through the winter.

Limes

If you garden in a region where you can grow limes, you're lucky, because this evergreen ornamental tree also offers fruit that can add a bit of tartness to your cooking…and your mojitos. Like other citrus, limes have lovely dark and glossy leaves and can be grown as shrubs or small trees. Standard limes reach 15 to 20 feet tall, but they are often grown to half that size on dwarf rootstock. They bear fruit in winter and late spring, although fruit can appear year-round in some areas. Their flavor ranges from fairly mild to extremely tart, depending on variety. Unfortunately, they can be very frost-sensitive. If you live in more cold-prone areas, provide winter protection.

Limes are completely mature when the fruit turns from green to yellow, but you can pick and eat them when they're green as soon as they reach the desired size.

CHOOSING A LIME: THE BASICS

The best lime for your garden depends on how you'll use the fruit and what will thrive in your garden. Some limes provide good juice; others are grown specifically for their culinary contribution. If you do a lot of Southeast Asian–style cooking, a 'Kieffer' lime might be right for you, and a 'Palestine Sweet' might be the best choice as an ingredient in Asian, Indian, and Latin American cooking. Consider taste as well; some limes are notably sweeter than others.

Limes

LiME VARiETiES

You will probably find the most common varieties, such as 'Bearss' or 'Mexican', on dwarf rootstock. Make sure the rootstock is actually a dwarfing type; plants grafted on semi-dwarfing rootstock can grow larger than you want.

BEARSS

(*or* 'Persian', 'Tahiti') Thorny lime, to 20 feet tall as a standard, with a rounded canopy. Tends to drop leaves in winter. Fruit is large for a lime. Fruits are traditional lime green when immature, maturing to a light yellow. Ripe 'Bearss' limes are juicy and seedless. Most fruits ripen from winter through spring, but a few stray fruits will ripen throughout the year.

KIEFFER

Shrublike shape and unique double leaves, which make it easy to identify. The leaves and rind are used in Thai and Cambodian cooking. Fruit ripens in spring, with warty looking green skin, and is extremely sour. Dwarf varieties are excellent container plants.

Limes continued

MEXICAN

(*or* 'Key' lime) Often used for drinks. Upright, thorny tree to 15 feet tall. Very sensitive to cold; best in warm climates. Small fruit is green or yellow-green and ripens fall to winter.

PALESTINE SWEET

(*or* 'Indian Lime') Tree is similar to 'Bearss' but shrubbier. Fruit ripens in fall or winter. Although used in some cuisines, its flavor can be too mild for those who appreciate the tartness of other limes.

Grapefruit

Grapefruit was a novelty tree and fruit less than 100 years ago, but today it's a breakfast staple. To grow it in your garden, however, you'll need some summer heat and patience. If conditions are right, you'll be able to eat this tart and tasty fruit directly off the tree. Those who grow it claim that this is how you'll get the best flavor.

The fruit grows in clusters that resemble bunches of grapes. But that's where the similarities between the two fruits end. The fruit is so much larger than a grape, at 4 to 6 inches in diameter, with yellow or yellow-orange skin and white to red flesh. Although it takes six months to a year to ripen, a grapefruit can remain on the tree for some time and still tastes great.

The tree itself is also large, growing 15 to 20 feet tall, and with age it can reach 30 feet or taller. Its rounded, spreading form is covered with large, thin, dark green leaves, and it has thorns. Even the grapefruit flowers are large, at about 2 inches across. A standard grapefruit, with its size, leaves, flowers, and distinctive fruit, truly makes a statement in your garden.

The best-tasting fruit develops in climates with hot summer days and warm nights, fairly high humidity, and sunny winter days with cool nights. Florida and Texas are some of the best grapefruit-growing regions. It can be grown in other citrus-friendly areas, but the fruit might not develop its rich color without intense summer heat. To increase summer heat, plant the tree against a sun-facing wall, which will reflect heat onto the plant.

Grapefruit can ripen in six months, but it usually takes at least nine months and up to a year. The peel color isn't always the best indicator of ripeness. After the fruit begins to feel heavy, your best bet is to pick a single fruit and taste it. Grapefruit can hold on the tree for months without affecting the fruit quality. Once harvested, fruit can be stored at room temperature for about a week and refrigerated for up to three weeks.

CHOOSING A GRAPEFRUIT: THE BASICS

Most people think of grapefruit in terms of flesh color: red, pink, or white. Color can vary, though, depending on the amount of summer heat to which the tree is exposed. A better deciding factor is whether the fruit has seeds or is seedless. As a general rule, a grapefruit with seeds tends to have a more intense flavor than a seedless variety.

You might occasionally find the grapefruit referred to as a shaddock. An ancestor of the grapefruit is the pummelo, which has a similar look and taste.

Grapefruits

GRAPEFRUIT VARIETIES

More and more choices are available for a variety of citrus-growing areas. Hybrids often don't need quite as much heat to produce fruit with good flavor. If your garden is small, look for the variety you want that has been grafted onto a true dwarfing rootstock and/or plant it in a large pot to limit the root zone and overall size; otherwise, the trees can outgrow your space.

COCKTAIL

Hybrid. Trees grow larger in warmer climates, smaller in cooler areas. Usually sold as a dwarf that reaches 8 feet tall. Extremely juicy fruit is smaller than true grapefruit, with unusual green- orange skin and seedy orange flesh. Can be eaten fresh, but also good candied and for marmalades and syrup. Fruit ripens from late fall through winter.

DUNCAN

True grapefruit. Old cultivar that is still popular. Strong-growing tree is considered cold-tolerant. Large, white-fleshed fruit is seedy but extremely juicy and flavorful. Fruit ripens fairly early and holds on the tree.

FLAME

True grapefruit. Large tree is more cold-tolerant than many others. Fruit rind is slightly pink; flesh is dark red and usually seedless. Fruit ripens from late fall through spring and hangs in clusters; can remain on tree, although flesh color can fade.

MARSH

(*or* 'Marsh Seedless') Florida favorite is more frost-sensitive than others. Fruit more oblong than round, with a light yellow peel; flesh is almost white and usually seedless. Juicy and not bitter; good fresh or used for juice. Fruit can remain on the tree for some time, but flavor will probably fade. Ripens in late fall through winter or spring, depending on location.

MELOGOLD

Hybrid that needs less heat than true grapefruit. Sister to 'Oro Blanco'. Large and spreading tree. Fruit is thick-skinned, large, heavy, and dark yellow, with seedless white flesh that is sweet and mild. Ripens fall through winter. Dwarf form is available, to 6–8 feet.

ORO BLANCO

Hybrid related to 'Melogold'. Large fruit with glossy, pale yellow skin, generally seedless flesh, and sweet flavor. Glossy leaves and large, fragrant white flowers. Does not need as much heat as a true grapefruit. Ripens fall through winter. Dwarf form is available.

Grapefruits continued

REDBLUSH

(*or* 'Ruby', 'Ruby Red') Seedless, medium-large grapefruit with red-tinged skin and red flesh that turns pink as the fruit ages. Color is best with heat. Good sweet-tart grapefruit flavor. Ripens winter through spring and can remain on the tree. Tree up to 25 feet; dwarf form is available.

RIO RED

(*or* 'Rio Star') Needs heat, but produces abundant fruit with reddish yellow skin. Seedless, with red flesh that is more sweet than tart. Good choice for juice. Ripens fall through winter. Dwarf form is available.

STAR RUBY

Fragile, compact tree will not tolerate cold or desert heat. Unreliable producer. Very red, seedless flesh. Dwarf form is available.

Kumquats

These small plants are easily mistaken for miniature orange trees, but kumquats are so much more than that. They might be small, but they are the hardiest trees of the citrus family, easily handling temperatures well below freezing. Their cold tolerance has encouraged breeders to cross them with other citrus, such as oranges and limes, to produce hardier versions of these favorites. Kumquats are the one citrus you eat rind and all; the taste of their tart flesh is deliciously offset by their sweet rinds.

Kumquats are one of the most decorative citrus. The tree is naturally attractive on its own, with a shrublike form; thick, long, dark green leaves; and fragrant white flowers that bloom in spring and summer. The tiny fruit, ranging in color from yellow to almost red, makes a striking accent on the plant. It's no wonder that they're often used as decorations, especially during the holiday season.

Their size also makes them ideal for small gardens and containers. Standard kumquats do not grow as tall as other citrus, usually reaching 6 to 15 feet; trees grown on dwarfing rootstocks reach about 4 feet. Hybrids top out at around 6 feet at most, and some are only half that size.

Fruit generally begins to ripen from fall (in the warmest areas) into winter. The fruit can remain on the tree up to a year without losing flavor, but it will tend to drop when temperatures spike.

CHOOSING A KUMQUAT: THE BASICS

Because kumquats are the most ornamental trees in the citrus family, choose a plant with a pleasing shape. If you're growing it as a tree, look for a strong central trunk. For a shrub or hedge, look for several strong branches. For espaliering, you'll want sturdy side branches. If garden space is limited, choose natural dwarf trees or plants grown on true dwarfing stock.

Kumquats

KUMQUAT VARIETIES

Although kumquats are growing in popularity for home gardeners, the number of available varieties is limited. Kumquat hybrids combine the flavor of other citrus with the cold hardiness and edible rinds of the kumquat.

FUKUSHU

Great for small gardens and containers. Naturally small tree, to 8 or 9 feet, with an attractive shape, round leaves, and no thorns. Orange rind is thin and sweet; deep orange flesh is tart. Fruit is relatively large compared to other kumquats, with some seeds.

MARUMI

Tree can reach 9 feet, with thick leaves and more thorns than many other kumquats. Smooth, yellow fruit has a sweet skin and seedy, tart flesh. More cold-tolerant than many kumquats.

MEIWA

Nearly thornless tree is a natural dwarf. Round orange fruit with thick peel is very juicy and sweet overall, and usually almost seedless. One of the best kumquats for eating fresh, but not as good for preserves. Does well in areas with cool summers.

Kumquats <small>continued</small>

Kumquat Hybrids

NAGAMI

Largest of the kumquats, at 15 feet, and thornless. Oval fruit is usually sold commercially. Takes summer heat as well as cold. More susceptible to mealybugs than other kumquats. A good choice for espaliers.

LIMEQUAT

A cross between 'Mexican' lime and kumquat. Tree is bushy and round. Good choice as a lime substitute as tree tolerates colder conditions. Tastes similar to lime, but the peel is edible. 'Eustis' and 'Lakeland' are tart and juicy; 'Tavares' is an overall better shaped plant. Ripens fall through spring.

ORANGEQUAT

Hybrid of 'Meiwa' kumquat and 'Satsuma' mandarin. Tolerates cold and requires less heat. 'Nippon' is popular. Fruit is dark orange, with tart flesh and a sweet rind; easy to eat fresh. Ripens winter through spring, but can remain on the tree.

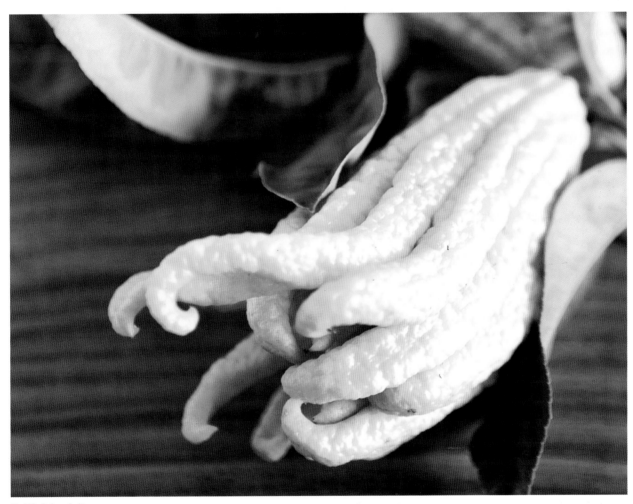

Buddha's hand citron

Citrons and Pommelos

Most citrus fruits are familiar to home gardeners and cooks, but a few unusual selections are recently beginning to show up in farmers' markets and groceries. Many of these are hybrids and are described here along with their parents. Some stand out on their own.

Citrons

CITRON VARIETIES

This older cultivated citrus variety is grown for its interesting fruit. The plant itself is small and thorny and extremely sensitive to cold weather. The fruit is large, with thick yellow skin. It bears fruit throughout the year, with the heaviest crop in the fall. A citron is an excellent choice for a container.

BUDDHA'S HAND

Rind has long, fingerlike extensions. Grown primarily as an ornamental novelty, but you can candy its peel.

ETHROG

(or 'Etrog') Fruit resembles a large lemon with ridges and warty skin. Some pulp, but it's completely dry. Rind can be candied. Used in the Jewish Feast of Tabernacles (Sukkot).

Pommelos

POMMELO VARIETIES

Also sold as pomelo, pummelo, and shaddock, this grapefruit relative is known for its huge fruits with thick rinds and membranes. Trees can be similar in size or slightly smaller than grapefruit trees with large leaves and flowers. The fruit is born in clusters and is heavy, so be vigilant about pruning to encourage strong branches.

Pommelos ripen in winter in the warmest areas and the season extends to early spring in cooler regions. Eating them is a challenge: you must peel them, separate the segments, and remove the membrane. The fruit is not quite as juicy as a grapefruit, and it ranges in taste from sweet to very sour. Fruit can stay on the tree for several months after it's ripe.

CHANDLER

The most popular variety. Pink flesh is sweet and relatively juicy. Can be espaliered.

REINKING

White-fleshed hybrid is somewhat sour.

TAHITIAN

Smaller tree. White-fleshed fruit's flavor is reminiscent of a lime.

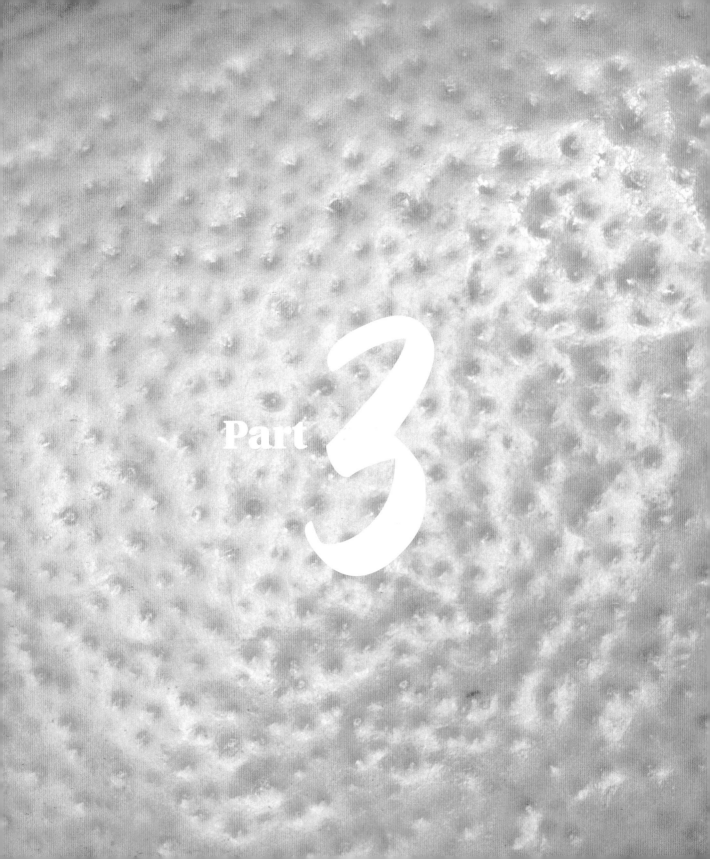

Part 3

Practicalities:
Long Live Your Orchard

Orchard Planting and Care

Whether you ordered your trees to be delivered through the mail or you will be picking them up at a local nursery, planting day is coming. The process of getting the ground ready to receive a tree can start years, days, or moments in advance. Improving the planting site starts with understanding your soil. Even if you are planting in pots, you need to understand how water and roots will tend to behave in the soil or planting medium.

Planting a multi-grafted apple

Dig in and feel your soil often. Clay soils feel slick, and sandy soils feel grainy.

Getting to Know Your Soil

The folks who study soils pay a lot of attention to a few main attributes. The first is soil texture: the relative amounts of sand, silt, and clay that make up the soil. A generic loam soil would have around 40 parts sand, 40 parts silt, and 20 parts clay and would likely be a nice spot to plant a tree.

Another important consideration is soil structure, or the way these different sized particles are arranged in the soil. Is the soil compacted? How deep are the various layers? It is easier to change the soil structure (through tillage, cover cropping, and other means) than it is to change the soil texture, but both can be improved.

The next key thing to consider is the soil pH. Fruit trees generally do best in the pH range 6.0–7.0.

Testing your soil is a great way to learn about its texture, structure, pH, and fertility. For a fee, most soil labs will offer suggestions on how to amend and improve your soil based on the crop you are planning to grow. Local agricultural extension agents, nurseries, or farmers can be great sources for where to send your soil for testing.

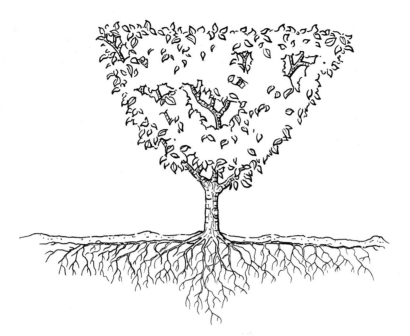

The most important roots are in the top 18 inches of soil and extend about 50 percent past the tree's canopy.

PREPARING THE PLANTING SITE

The approach you take in preparing your soil can, in large part, determine how you will need to care for the soil throughout the life of the tree. If you focus on feeding the soil throughout your garden and work to build a healthy soil structure, your trees won't be as dependent on you for their every need.

Many gardeners strive to create a rich, loose soil in the planting hole and load it up with compost and fertilizers at planting time. The problem with this approach is two-fold. First, water doesn't move very well between soils of different textures inside and outside the planting site, and the root zone can end up being too moist or too dry if the surrounding soil differs from that in the planting hole. Second, roots can get lazy if all the food they need is close by—that is, they won't spread as far looking for nutrients. A tree with a more extensive root system will be healthier and more resistant to dry spells, will have better access to nutrients, and will ultimately produce more and tastier fruit.

If you don't prepare the garden soil before you plant, you can end up with a tree planted in ground that has all the drawbacks of one planted in a container, without any of the benefits. The best idea is to enhance the soil throughout as large an area as possible. The goal is to give your tree's roots free reign to explore far and wide for nutrients and water, rather than being attached to a feedbag or IV drip by its side. Think of it as free-range fruit.

You might have been told that a tree's root system mirrors the crown, or spread, of the tree. In fact, for most trees including fruit trees, the most important roots are in the top 18 inches of soil and extend about 50 percent past the tree's canopy. This first horizon of the soil is where the mix of oxygen, moisture, and nutrients are optimal for root health. If your garden is blessed with good dirt, you might decide to do little or nothing to enhance the soil before planting. On the other hand, you can improve your soil in a number of ways, as you will soon discover.

DEALING WITH DRAINAGE ISSUES

Your understanding of how water moves in your soil is essential before you decide how and what to plant. Few fruit trees thrive in waterlogged soils, so first determine whether that is the situation in your garden. The simplified, unscientific, version of this test requires that you dig a couple of holes around your yard and fill them with water. If it takes the better part of day for that water to disappear, you should plan to improve the drainage, plant in containers, or plant something else in the most poorly drained areas. If your hole looks like beach sand, you might need to improve the water retention. In both cases, adding compost is a good start.

Although most roots tend to stay fairly close to the surface, deeper roots sitting in waterlogged soils can invite pests and disease. You can improve drainage in many ways, from the extreme to the fairly tame. At the more extreme end of the spectrum, install drainage pipes that direct the water to a dry well (a buried barrel, filled with gravel or left empty and fitted with a sump pump), another low spot, a storm drain, or a collection area. How far apart you place drainage pipes will be determined again by how water moves through the soil. In

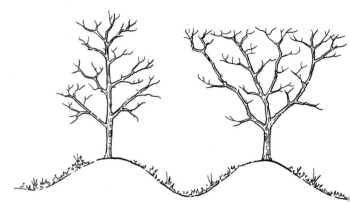

Trees can be planted in mounds of soil in wet areas.

heavier soils, pipes should be placed closer together. A single pipe running close to a row of trees and into a small dry well can actually be very effective at improving drainage, and it's not that difficult to install.

Mounding the soil can add interest to your landscape design and can be an effective way to enhance roots' quality of life. Picture a series of ridges and valleys (also called berms and swales) with a line of trees planted at the high points and herbs and vegetables covering the slopes. If you import soil to form the berms, make an effort to integrate it with the indigenous soil. To do this, spread a few inches of your new soil on the surface and work it into the existing soil with a rototiller or by hand. Then add more imported soil on top to create a higher mound. This way, the roots and water will spread through a more natural transition between the new and native soil layers.

Peaches and nectarines are the most sensitive to poor drainage. If your soil has drainage problems, your best bet is to make as many improvements as you can and to choose fruits that are the most tolerant of wet feet, such as pears, plums, and apples on selected rootstocks.

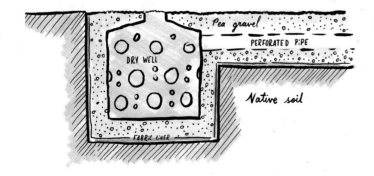

DRY WELL

Pea gravel

PERFORATED PIPE

DRY WELL

Native soil

FABRIC LINER

Testing soil percolation rates

A well-fitted scythe is by far the most elegant way to mow a cover crop.

Amendments and Mulching

You can correct for deficiencies in your soil in several ways, depending on what you discover in your soil assessment. If you do not observe deficiencies and your soil seems ideal, you might need to do little other than provide mulch and regular water.

COVER CROPS

Cover cropping is the practice of planting a crop for the purpose of improving the soil. Plants in the bean and pea family (legumes) have the wonderful ability to team up with soil bacteria and create nitrogen for themselves right out of thin air. Through this special relationship, nodules on the plant roots actually take nitrogen that is in the air part of the soil, which would otherwise be inaccessible to plants, and convert it into a usable plant food. We can "harvest" these nitrogen nuggets by severing the plant from its roots before it starts to set seeds and has chance to use that nitrogen for itself.

The vegetative growth of your cover crop can be cut and removed for composting or tilled back into the soil as what is referred to as a green manure. Depending on the cover crop you choose, allow at least a few weeks for the green manure to break down before planting something else, because the soil's biological activities will be occupied decomposing that organic matter. Many seed companies these days offer multi-seed blends for cover crops and provide information on which are best suited for your situation. Local agricultural suppliers or nurseries can be a great resource for seed and information about planting a successful cover crop.

Studies have shown that inoculating your seed with specific beneficial soil microorganisms before planting can greatly increase the nitrogen production of legumes. Your seed supplier should be able to provide a powdered inoculant that contains the right mix of organisms for the type of seeds you want to plant. To use the inoculant, in a small bowl or bucket, moisten small batches of seed and sprinkle the inoculant over the seed to coat it well. Sow that seed in moist, not wet, soil and maintain adequate moisture through germination. I can personally attest to the value of planting cover crops.

In 2004, my wife and I bought a house in downtown Napa that had a tired, old crabgrass lawn for a front yard. The garden I was tending at the time had a shiny new Kubota tractor, and that fall I drove it home and tilled up the grass. (A rented walk-behind tiller would have done the job, but where's the drama in that?) We raked and picked out all the clumps of crabgrass that we could find and spread compost, oyster shell flour, and rock dust, and then sowed a cover crop of bell beans, vetch, field peas, and oats. In early spring, when the cover crop was waist high and my neighbors started signing a petition (not really, but my cover crop was actually a great ice-breaker), I brought the tractor home and tilled again. In those few months, the hard, compacted soil that had mainly functioned as a parking spot in earlier years was already teeming with worms and looked like good garden soil.

We planted a peach, two nectarines, two plums, and a pluot as well as various oreganos and thymes, euphorbia, penstemon, salvias, bunch grasses, and New Zealand flax. That garden continues to thrive under the current maintenance plan that consists of occasionally running the drip irrigation system.

Because we were converting all the lawn to a garden, we had a unique opportunity to give the whole space the same treatment. I think this really helped get that garden off to a great start and is probably (along with plant selection) what has allowed it to thrive with very low maintenance.

COMPOST

It's hard not to think of well-made compost as a panacea in the garden. Compost is a mild, slow-release fertilizer and soil conditioner that increases organic matter content, nutrient holding ability, and biological activity in your soil. And you can make it at home.

Clay soils tend to hold plenty of nutrients, but they are also heavy and are not the most hospitable places for plant roots. Compost incorporated into the top layer of a clay soil can help open up the pore spaces in the soil and make nutrients, as well

When these guys move into your compost, you know it is cooling down and almost ready to use.

as air and water, more accessible to plants. If you garden in sandy soil, the prescription is the same: add compost. Compost will help sandy soils hold onto water and nutrients that would tend to move quickly away from the root zone.

Keep a few points in mind when applying compost in the garden, and particularly around fruit trees. First, make sure that the compost you are using, whether it is store-bought or homemade, is well decomposed. Ideal compost should look like forest soil, and you should not be able to identify its components, such as whole banana peels or bits of shredded plant material. Mixing in unfinished compost can tie up nutrients in the soil and create an environment ripe for pests and disease.

As wonderful as compost is, you can overdo it. A common mistake is applying a heavy mulch of compost right up to and around the base of a fruit tree. This again brings up the issue of how water moves through soils of different textures. The compost sitting on top of your garden soil can end up becoming very sodden and anaerobic (absent of available oxygen). Compost or any other mulch that is touching the trunk of the tree can trap moisture against the bark, causing rot and disease.

To make compost that is of particular benefit to fruit trees, aim to encourage the growth of fungal organisms over bacterial organisms in the pile. Many books thicker than this one are dedicated solely to the topic of compost, so I won't spend too much time on it here. The straightforward way to make fungal-dominated compost is simply to add a bit more brown stuff when building your pile. Wood chips and dry leaves are probably the most readily available ingredients. Start by layering a few inches of woody material and then alternate layers of green waste, woody stuff, and fresh manure. Make the pile at least 3-by-3-by-3 feet, and make sure the browns outnumber the greens. Keep the whole thing moist, turn it regularly, and before long you will have a great supply of compost mulch for your trees.

A compost thermometer can be a handy tool for keeping tabs on how your pile is progressing.

Mixing blended organic fertilizer with native soil before refilling the planting hole

GYPSUM

Along with compost, adding mined gypsum can be helpful for opening up compacted soils. Spread 3 to 4 pounds of gypsum over 100 square feet of soil surface annually, and water it in. One of the nice things about gypsum is that it does not need to be incorporated into the soil to be effective. In fact, you should apply gypsum only on the surface of the soil, because some negative reactions can occur if it is mixed into the lower soil horizons. Spread it around other perennials and in you garden beds, and during the next few years, you should see improved water percolation and plant growth.

OYSTER SHELL FLOUR

Calcium helps plants build strong cell walls and resist disease, and it is important for the development of healthy roots, leaves, flowers, and fruit. Along with stunted growth, one indication of low calcium is heavy fruit drop. Crushed oyster shells can provide a slow-release calcium fertilizer in the soil, and like gypsum, they tend to show their benefits over time. One of the better sources of organic calcium, oyster shell flour, can also be spread on the surface to discourage slugs and snails. The powder can be added to the compost pile, raising the nutrient content of your compost and making the calcium more available. Apply 1 to 2 pounds per 100 square feet annually for mildly calcium-deficient soils. If you can't find oyster shell, crab shell flour or regular agricultural lime can be used.

BLENDED ORGANIC FERTILIZERS

The fertilizer aisle of your local garden store can be a confusing place. You'll see a lot of numbers staring you in the face, and it isn't always clear what makes one fertilizer good for fruit trees and another one good for vegetables or azaleas. The good news is that in most cases your fruit trees won't need much in the way of supplemental fertilizer, especially if you are mulching with compost. Citrus is the main exception, and meeting their specific fertility needs can significantly increase citrus fruit production and health.

I hold a bias toward organically derived fertilizers; I find them to be mild, fairly long lasting, and generally not disruptive to the

Notice the white hyphae (filaments) of the beneficial soil bacteria actinomycetes

other biological systems I am trying to employ in support of my fruit trees. Blended organic fertilizers are made from a wide range of animal, plant, and mineral sources and can also include cultured soil microbes. Although their effectiveness remains somewhat unproven, cultured microbes can function to increase the biological activity in your soil, making for better overall nutrient availability and soil health.

ROCK POWDERS

Minerals and trace elements are at least as important as nitrogen, phosphorus, and potassium (N-P-K) when it comes to the development of high-quality fruit. This is my conclusion after years of experimenting with various combinations of soil amendments. We often focus on the nutrient needs of our plants, forgetting the contribution that minerals and trace elements make to healthy soil biology, pest and disease resistance, and flavor development. The minerals in rock powders are collected from many sites, and for this reason I like to alternate products, applying Azomite (silica clay) one year and glacial rock dust the next, for example. For small trees, annually in the fall or spring, I scratch 1 to 2 pounds into the top few inches of soil or directly under the drip emitters in my irrigation system.

WOODCHIP MULCH

In the fruit tree plantings I've encountered, trees surrounded by a steady supply of mulch usually require the lowest maintenance. Of particular benefit are chips derived from smaller diameter (less than 2 inches) branches from deciduous trees. Sometimes called ramial woodchips, this material can help create an ideal environment for beneficial fungal activity, and it provides several essential nutrients. If you were thinking about getting your trees a birthday present, this is sure to please.

If you can't find mulch made from small-diameter branches, any wood mulch can be beneficial. Do try to avoid using black walnut (*Juglans nigra*) or cedar (*Thuja species*) chips on young trees, because these can have allelopathic, or growth suppressing, effects.

COMPOST TEA

Like a good cup of herbal tea when you're feeling a little under the weather, a tasty batch of compost tea can brighten your fruit tree's day. As a foliar spray, compost tea provides nutrients as well as some protection from fungal disease. As a soil drench, aerobic compost tea is like an energy drink for tree roots.

Whether you use a dedicated brewer or fish tank bubbler taped to the bottom of a bucket, you can make quality compost tea at home. If you are using city water, fill the bucket the night before or bubble air through it for an hour or so to release the chlorine before adding compost to the water. Add the compost loose and strain it later, or make a compost tea bag using pantyhose or something similar to hold the material. Aerate the brew for 24 hours, and then apply it to the tree with a watering can or pump sprayer.

FERMENTED PLANT TEAS

Like compost tea, fermented plant teas can be a great free source of micronutrients and a healing drink for plant roots. Unlike compost tea, however, it should not be used on leaves; the anaerobic fermentation process can cultivate organisms that are great for the soil but can bring disease if applied to leaves.

To make plant tea, fill a watertight trashcan with as much plant material as you can gather. Comfrey, stinging nettle, and horsetail are all good choices. Add some willow bark, which can help heal roots that have been damaged by burrowing rodents or transplanting. Fill the can with water, place a loose-fitting lid on top, and give the brew a vigorous stir every day for three weeks or more. The stink will let you know that this is a nutritious brew, so don't set it up outside your bedroom window. Dilute your fermented tea in up to 10 parts of clean water and use it to water your trees. Experiment with dilution rates as strong as 1 part water to 1 part tea, down to 10 parts water to 1 part tea.

Planting in Ground

Bare-root fruit trees are usually planted during the dormant season, when it's still cool outside. If possible, schedule tree delivery or pickup as late as possible in the season. The sweet spot would be a dry spell a couple of weeks before the spring push of new leaves, flowers, and roots. (Just ask your nursery to schedule that dry spell for ya!) Stone fruit, and particularly the various plum cultivars, tend to be the first to emerge in spring, so get those in first. Citrus roots are sensitive to disturbance and are not usually sold as bare-root plants.

Planting a bare-root pear: roots are spread over a cone of soil in the planting hole.

After you receive your trees, try to plant them as soon as possible. If your schedule or the weather doesn't allow for that, prop them up at a 45-degree angle and cover the roots with loose soil or mulch—this is called heeling in. Just don't let the trees wallow in limbo for too long. Also, make irrigation decisions before you begin planting, so that any trenching you need to do will not disturb young tree roots.

It would be tough to argue that planting day is better than harvest day, but it is at least a close second. All the time you put into selecting varieties and preparing the site has brought you to this critical moment. The planting part is actually pretty simple.

In late spring and early summer, you'll often find a good selection of common fruit trees in 5 gallon or larger pots. Many nurseries these days sell larger fruit trees in containers or boxes of 24 inches or larger. Although buying a larger tree can be a nice option, you'll probably find fewer selections available, and the varieties offered tend to be the more common ones. However, if you find a variety you are looking for with a good branch structure and are after a mature-looking landscape with bigger trees, go for it.

How you plant container-grown trees is similar to the bare-root planting method, except you can probably count on having better weather, since you won't be constrained by the time frame of bare-root trees.

PLANTING A BARE-ROOT TREE

1. Dig a hole wide and deep enough to accommodate the roots of your tree, and form a mound of soil in the center. If you are using a stake to support the tree, set it just off the center of this mound and deep enough to feel stable when you pull firmly on it. If your soil is very poor and you plan to amend the planting area, make the planting hole as wide as possible, up to 6 feet or more in diameter, and add amendments to the soil you've removed before adding it back into the hole.

2. Choose an orientation for your tree and spread the roots evenly around the mound so that they are directed down at about a 45-degree angle. Adjust and firm the roots against the mound so that the tree will sit on a solid base with no air pockets.

3. Blend any amendments (mild organic fertilizers, well-finished compost, and so on) into the fill dirt, and gently add that soil back in around the roots, double-checking that you are not covering the graft union with soil. As you refill the soil in the hole, firm the first few shovels full around the roots to avoid air pockets. After refilling, the soil level should be just above the spot where the roots emanate from the trunk. Adjust the planting depth so that the final soil grade will meet the trunk of your new tree about ½ inch above the highest roots.

4. Step back and make sure the tree is straight and is in the right spot.

5. Press firmly on the soil right up to the trunk with your hands, and then form a ridge of soil around the edges of the hole and away from the trunk; this is a little moat to keep water from being disbursed too far from the tree.

6. For small spaces, and depending on the branch structure of the tree, your next step is to get out your loppers and make a clean cut on the trunk, a couple of inches above where you want the tree's lowest branches to emerge.

7. If you are using a stake or trellis, tie the trunk to the stake or trellis wire.

8. The final step in any planting project is to water the plant in. This will force air pockets out of the soil and help introduce roots to soil.

PLANTING A CONTAINER-GROWN TREE

1. If space allows, dig a planting hole that is two to three times as wide as the container. Try to create a flat base of undisturbed soil so that the root mass will be well supported and less likely to settle much after planting.

2. Use a digging fork or other tool to fracture the soil around the perimeter of the hole.

3. If the tree is not fully rooted in to its container (it feels loose when you gently tug on the trunk), you will need to take care to avoid having the rootball fall apart while planting. Consider cutting off the bottom of the pot (I use a battery-powered Sawzall), setting the tree in its place, and carefully sliding the pot over the tree; or cut up one edge and peel the pot away. Remove the tree from its pot, and lightly loosen the planting mix outside the root ball. If you see a dense tangle of roots at the base of the pot, tease or prune those apart.

HiGH-DENSiTY PLANTiNG

Ed Laivo (pictured here with a 4-in-1 cherry planting) helped to introduce the concept of high-density planting.

If you want a simple solution for a longer, more diverse fruit harvest, planting multiple trees in one hole is a great way to squeeze more variety into your garden. Space three or four trees 12 to 24 inches apart and plant each as you would a single tree. A trio of early, mid- and late season varieties is like having a single tree with a harvest window up to three times longer than normal.

No book on growing fruit trees in small spaces would be complete without mentioning Backyard Orchard Culture, as outlined by Dave Wilson Nursery. The goal of this method is to achieve a long harvest of tree-ripe fruit through the planting of multiple trees and even multiple species in a single planting hole. With summer pruning, trees are kept smaller than their rootstock would indicate.

I have had good success following these methods and recommend that you experiment with these techniques. It took some getting used to, but I've come to appreciate the look of three or four trees planted in the same hole and trained like a single open-center tree.

Planting in Containers

Physically, there isn't a huge difference between planting in a pot and planting in the ground. Look for a tree variety that will naturally stay small and that can be maintained to a manageable size with pruning. Choose the largest container that makes sense for your space. A 15 gallon container is about the smallest size in which you should plant a tree.

Thick-walled ceramic pots heat up slowly and release that heat overnight, which is great for growing varieties that require a climate a bit warmer than yours. Thin plastic pots are lighter and easier to move around, but they also tend to heat up the soil inside more quickly and dry it out, requiring more attention on your part. Make sure the container you choose

has a drainage hole, and try to keep it unobstructed. As always, be sure to provide regular water.

Fill your container with a soil mix that drains well and isn't too heavy, and amend it with organic fertilizers. You can lighten your soil blend by adding up to one-third vermiculite or cedar shavings to the mix.

Trees in containers can't send out roots far and wide to scavenge for water and nutrients the way a tree planted in the ground does, so keep a close eye on those needs and plan to repot your tree every three to five years, depending on the container size and tree growth.

Planting a kumquat in a terracotta pot

Irrigation Systems

Many options are available for getting water to your trees. Automated irrigation systems provide a sense of confidence (sometimes false) that your trees are regularly getting the water they need. Watering by hand, however, lets you be sure that your trees have been given a good drink, and it gets you outside and looking at your trees on a regular basis (a good thing). Whether or not you install a timed irrigation system is largely a matter of personal preference. Do you like the ritual of grabbing a cup of coffee and watering your yard? Or are you someone who travels a lot and whose friends don't like to babysit plants?

However you decide to water your trees, the key component of the system is you. If you install an automated system, avoid the temptation to "set it and forget it." Check regularly that the physical parts of the system are functioning well (no disconnected hoses, clogged emitters, or other problems) and that the run times are sufficient to get the soil evenly moist, but not soggy.

Established trees growing in the ground will require much less water than young trees or those planted in containers, and they need to be watered less often than your lawn. Some of us tend to be more "enthusiastic" than others when it comes to watering (my neighbor waters her sidewalk), so make sure you're not overdoing it. I have seen many more problems as a result of folks watering their trees too much than too little. Trees and soil do not use time clocks, so you don't have to provide the exact same amount of water week in and week out; you just need to maintain a reasonable amount of moisture in the soil. In addition, trees don't stop working after harvest, so don't quit on 'em too soon. In fact, well-timed irrigations after harvest can be essential for good fruit set the following year.

Where you put the water is almost as important as how much you water. Picture the roots of your tree spreading out in a shallow radius around the trunk. This is the zone where you will apply water. Remember that the most important roots are in the top layer of soil and extend about 50 percent past the tree's canopy. I commonly see irrigation lines with a single emitter placed directly at the trunk of a tree. A much better layout would be a ring around the tree's drip line (the area under the edge of the tree's canopy) with five or six emitters or a microsprinkler with a similar radius. If you are watering by hand, focus on this zone, or consider forming two ridges of soil to create a kind of moat toward the perimeter of the tree's canopy that you can fill with water.

Pests and Diseases

Too often, when trouble strikes a garden, whether in the form of an invasion of pests, an outbreak of disease, or even disappointing fruit production, gardeners turn to chemical controls. But those bring their own issues, including unintentional destruction of beneficial insects and the residual remains of the chemicals on your fruit. Instead, consider starting with the gentlest approaches, beginning with easy preventive measures; turn to harsher remedies only if these don't work.

THE HEALTHY GARDEN

A healthy garden starts with healthy plants. Before choosing a tree at the nursery, make sure that it is in good shape. Check everything, from roots to leaves, looking for problems: withered or circling roots, cuts and nicks in the bark, and malformed or pale leaves. Give it a shake to remove any pests that are hiding it its leaves.

At home, give your new tree optimal growing conditions. Choose a planting site that receives the appropriate amount of sunlight. Amend the soil if it isn't ideal, and provide sufficient nutrients, air circulation, and shelter from harsh climate conditions that might affect its growth. Take your time preparing the planting hole to give the tree the best chance to settle into its new spot.

During the growing season, provide sufficient water and nutrients, and add mulch to help repress weeds and retain moisture in the soil. One of the best things you can do to prevent problems is to keep you garden clean and tidy. Remove dead and diseased branches, fallen fruits, weeds, and

iRRiGATiON SYSTEM COMPONENTS

If you decide to install an irrigation system, do a little research first or consult an irrigation specialist to help you choose the best system for your trees and garden. Every system setup requires unique components, and it can get complicated, but a few components are common in most systems.

TIMER A timer regulates the watering schedule via a simple battery-powered, hose-end timer attached to a spigot or a more permanent hard-wired controller connected to a series of valves. A timer with the ability to program multiple stations will control more than one valve and allow you to expand the system.

FILTER Most irrigation systems require a filter. You'll need at least a 120-mesh filter for a drip system, and misters and drip tape require a 200-mesh filter. The cost of the filter is worth it, because you avoid the hassle of dealing with clogged emitters. One large filter can serve multiple valves. Install the filter in an accessible spot so that if you notice a dip in pressure or flow, you can easily clean it.

VALVES Hose-end timers combine a clock and a valve in a single unit. For plumbed systems in residential landscapes, ¾-inch or I-inch valves are the most common. It pays to invest in a quality product that can be serviced if components get clogged.

PRESSURE REGULATOR Drip emitters will function only at their listed gallons per hour if the water pressure is within the specified range—usually from 10 psi to 20 psi (pounds per square inch). Microsprinklers have a wider range, from as low as 15 psi up to 60 psi. Even if you are not sure whether you have high water pressure, a regulator will help the system run smoothly.

TUBING AND PIPING With a hose-end timer, you can immediately attach a line of ½-inch poly tubing and run that out to your trees. This type of tubing is connected by compression fittings and does not require glue. With plumbed valves, run PVC pipe from the valve to individual watering devices at each tree or to a central point, and then attach poly tubing. Fittings such as T's, elbows, and closures will help you lay out an effective design to provide water for your trees. All your trees can likely be irrigated on the same circuit.

EMITTERS AND SPRINKLERS By installing a T fitting into a line of solid ½-inch tubing, you can attach a shorter length of inline drip hose in a circle around your tree. This type of hose has emitters installed in it at regular intervals. You can also plug emitters into solid tubing. Microsprinklers can be connected to ½-inch tubing or PVC. Check the flow rate and number of emitters or sprinklers to get a read on how much water you are actually giving your trees.

The plant diversity and natural air circulation in this vigorous garden help to keep pests and diseases at bay.

encroaching plants. Keep an eye on your tree even before fruit forms to discover any problems early on. At the end of the growing season, remove fallen leaves and fruit and continue to keep the area around the tree clean and weed-free.

DEALING WITH PESTS

If your trees are troubled by pests, from insects to animals, start with the simplest solutions. In some cases, that might be as easy as waiting for predators—birds, predatory insects, and the like—to arrive to deal with an insect problem. You can also decide, especially in the case of animal damage, that

you are willing to share some of your produce. If the damage is greater than you can tolerate, however, you might need to take more steps.

Your first choice should be physical controls. Sometimes, you can simply handpick and destroy pests such as snails or caterpillars to keep them in check. Some insects can be eliminated by knocking them off the tree with a strong spray of water or a solution of water with 10 percent dishwashing liquid (one that's environmentally friendly and not antibacterial). Fences, netting, sticky barriers, and barrier collars that wrap around the base of trees can deter some pests.

Pheromone traps, or sticky traps, are tent-shaped traps baited with an attracting dose of the target insect's sex hormone. The insect is attracted to the hormone, and as it investigates the source, it gets stuck on the sticky surface of the trap and dies. Sticky cards and pheromone traps, when used properly, are quite effective against their targeted insects. Blue cards are effective against thrips and leaf miners, and yellow sticky traps attract aphids and whiteflies.

Another similar approach, pheromone disruption, can also be effective. Small twist-ties are infused with the pheromone scent of the targeted pest (codling moth on apples, for example) and hung in the trees. Apparently, the elevated levels of the sex pheromone confuse the males of the population and they are unable to find a mate, greatly reducing future populations.

Nature is incredibly adept at keeping populations under control, and you can use this to your advantage. Birds, amphibians, bats, and garter snakes can help keep your entire garden, not just your fruit trees, free of problem pests. Add bird-attracting plants; encourage frogs and toads by providing water and cool, moist hiding spots (overturned containers are a favorite); and provide habitat for bats and snakes to bring these animals into the garden. Of course, birds might want to eat your fruit as much as you do, but simple controls such as netting and providing alternative food sources, or simply realizing that you can share, will help you live in harmony with the animals in your garden.

Instead of just fighting the so-called bad insects, encourage or introduce the beneficial types in your garden. Beneficial insects are your little garden helpers, and a surprising number of them are readily available to help. The most familiar is probably the ladybug, or lady beetle (and with more than 100 species, you might not recognize them all). Other beneficial insects include the assassin bugs, damsel bugs, various beetles, lacewings, parasitic nematodes, pirate bugs, stink bugs, soldier beetles, and parasitic wasps. Trichogramma parasitic wasps are a class of tiny beneficial insects that can be released on farms and gardens to attack many caterpillar pests such as codling moth. Both syrphid flies and tachinid flies are also helpful in the garden, as are spiders. Learn to recognize these

Ants are farming scale insects on a fig leaf. Keep ants off trees by applying a sticky barrier (such as the Tanglefoot brand) around the trunk.

A syrphid fly, also called a hoverfly, visits a flower in the vegetable garden. In their larval stage, these flies prey upon aphids and other garden pests.

insects, and consider adding plants that provide food and shelter for them (for example, yarrow, lovage, and fennel attract syrphid flies). They will not only prey on insects such as thrips and aphids, but they help to pollinate plants as they feed on pollen and nectar.

As a last resort, turn to pesticides. The world of pesticides is rapidly changing, as more and new varieties become available. Some natural pesticides are derived from plants, animals, or minerals or use a naturally occurring biological method to produce the desired results. Synthetic types are made from compounds not found in nature. Natural does not necessarily mean that it's harmless, however. Always read labels thoroughly so you understand what insects are affected (including beneficial ones); how harmful it might be to other plants, people, or pets; and precisely how to apply it and how to dispose of it.

Natural pesticides include *Bacillus thuringiensis* (Bt), diatomaceous earth, insecticidal soap, neem extract, biodegradable pyrethrins (an extract of chrysanthemum), spinosad (derived from soil-dwelling bacteria), and sulfur. You'll also find horticultural oils, oils made from foods (or make your own), and neem oil. Use the latter with care, because it is toxic to fish.

PREVENTING DISEASES

Plant diseases, which are caused by fungi, bacteria, or viruses, can be as difficult to control as human diseases after they've taken hold and symptoms appear. And as with humans, good prevention is the best way to keep disease from attacking a plant. Start by choosing disease-free plants; if they are certified disease-free, so much the better. If you garden in an area where certain diseases are common, such as fireblight or verticillium wilt, look for disease-resistant varieties. This does not guarantee that a tree will not develop the disease, however.

Keeping your garden healthy is particularly important in preventing diseases. In addition to keeping your garden clean and well tended, you should remove and destroy any parts of a tree or surrounding plants that are affected by disease. When pruning, sterilize your tools in a 10 percent bleach solution (1 part bleach, 9 parts water) between each pruning cut, or simply spray them with a can of Lysol.

Again, if you need to apply a disease control substance, such as dormant sprays, read the labels carefully before choosing a product. Copper compounds are often used for diseases that affect foliage, such as brown rot, fireblight, and peach leaf curl. Lime sulfur is also a good dormant spray for brown rot, peach leaf curl, and scab. Copper soap and garlic-based fungicides are useful for controlling rust and black spot. Neem oil is used primarily as a pesticide, but it can control some foliar diseases such as scab and rust. Sulfur, a familiar control for long-time gardeners, controls a number of pest and disease problems, but it should not be used at the same time as horticultural oils, or in hot weather. New products are being manufactured, so check carefully for what is available.

Dormant spraying can mean
less time spent worrying about
pests and diseases.

Pruning and Training

Pruning is perhaps the most up close and personal that we get with plants. It takes time to develop a relationship with any living thing to a point where it feels okay, let alone beneficial, to lop off major limbs. It can actually be paralyzing (for the gardener, not the tree). More than one student of mine has stood, saw in hand, for an uncomfortably long period of time staring at a tree, waiting for inspiration to strike. This has helped foster my belief that each of us has a tendency to be either an

**The pruning kit, in order of use:
folding saw, loppers, and shears**

aggressive or a timid pruner, and we would all do well to move a bit toward the center.

I love preparing for a day of pruning—gathering snacks, wrapping a sandwich in a handkerchief, and brewing a thermos full of coffee or tea. I don the appropriate clothing (a belt, layers, and nothing too loose that will snag on branches), look over my notes from last year, and sharpen my tools. A certain amount of ceremony is involved, particular to the first pruning session of the year. I don't want it to pass mindlessly; I want to savor the smells and sounds of that opening day as I move from tree to tree.

I also want to share this with someone. I love to prune alone, but I can't think of a better way to share time with a friend, new or old, than by spending a few hours working over some trees together. As you build up to a confident pruning rhythm, it feels great to be able to step back and look at the form that is unfolding with two sets of eyes, or to get a consult on a particularly difficult cut. "Does this thing want to go open center?" naturally leads to, "You serious about going back to school?"

Suckers ready for removal on a dwarf 'Bonanza' peach

Fruit Tree Pruning Basics

Most of us will need to study, practice, observe, and repeat to get to a place of confidence with our pruning skills. And because the clock is set to tree-time, we just have to cram as much pruning as we can into each season and try to stick around long enough to see the results. I suggest you read over the basics here, but don't get overly bogged down by the rules. For the most part, you learn to prune by pruning. Learn to identify cuts from previous years and see what sort of growth response they elicited.

There are as many different approaches to pruning as there are sets of pruning shears in this world, but some goals and principles are common to most. It will be difficult to get past the first few cuts if you don't have some objectives in place before you start. At the least, make sure you have a game plan that considers the overall tree form and where that particular tree tends to set its fruit. Combine that with an understanding of the general principles of healthy pruning and you will be set up for years of enjoyment and delicious crops.

Traditionally, pruning is a winter activity, and you already know that I love a good winter pruning session. My hope is that you will come away from this reading with a sense that pruning can be a useful part of the year-round care of your trees. The simplified version of the story is this: with winter pruning, we are primarily interested in encouraging new growth (tipping cuts) or making major structural changes (removal cuts). Summer pruning is used to maintain a tree's size after it has filled, or is approaching, its allotted space (stopping cuts). Winter pruning tends to dominate the early years of a tree's life, while summer pruning can take the lead after the form is established. For the home orchardist with limited space, a plan for summer pruning can mean the difference between having space for one tree or a dozen.

More than one friend of mine thinks of winter pruning season as the most wonderful time of the year. I tend to agree, especially having just come inside from a sunny, 65°F pruning session in the hills above the Napa Valley, California. It is mid-January, and I lack the willpower required to hold my excitement inside. Much has been said and written about gardening as a meditative art, and nowhere is that more true than in the dormant orchard. As a professional gardener, it is difficult for me to get to that state in the same way in summer, surrounded by so much growth, activity, and heat. Even as I've embraced summer pruning as perhaps the more important practice for fruit trees in small spaces, nothing compares to slipping into that dormant pruning mindset.

BASIC PRUNING PRINCIPLES

Check out the beautiful crotch angles on this apple.

First, always maintain cleanliness. If you are removing diseased plant material, be sure to disinfect your tools before moving to another branch or tree. All you need is a small spray bottle with a 10 percent bleach solution and a clean rag. Keep diseased plant material out of your compost pile.

Seek balance. Balance is an important principle that is as good for pruning as it is everywhere else in life. Try to encourage even growth around the tree, keeping the overall tree form in mind. Visit your tree often and combine winter and summer pruning to keep growth in harmony.

Work the angles. Acute crotch angles tend to be weak unions that are highly susceptible to breakage, and they are usually out of sync with the overall form of the tree. Vertical branches tend to remain very vegetative and vigorous. As a branch drops to below horizontal, it tends to become weak and fruit productivity declines. Branches that emanate from the trunk from horizontal up to a 45-degree angle tend to be fruitful and strong.

Prune for multiple leaders. Many fruit trees exhibit apical dominance, in which the growth tip or tallest branch of the tree releases a growth-suppressing hormone that inhibits growth in the buds below it. Cherries, pears, apples, and plums show the strongest tendency toward apical dominance. Pruning to multiple leaders can keep each leader branch in balance, as each competes for dominance. Summer pruning can also help, as can training to lower angles or allowing the weight of fruit to pull a branch tip down.

WHY WE PRUNE

Especially in small spaces, pruning can be an essential practice in maintaining balance in your overall landscape. We prune fruit trees for several reasons:

TO CREATE A SOLID FRAMEWORK FOR FRUIT PRODUCTION
A healthy structure will allow sufficient light penetration and airflow within and around the tree.

TO HELP BALANCE THE CROP LOAD Pruning can reduce the time we spend thinning fruit and can encourage fruit production.

TO REMOVE SUCKERS AND WATER SPROUTS Suckers are shoots that grow from the roots and should be removed as close to their origin as possible. Water sprouts are similar upright shoots that grow along a trees' branches. These vigorous shoots should be removed or trained to a lower orientation. They are called water sprouts because they often indicate that your soil has a drainage problem.

TO REMOVE THE FOUR Ds Pruning removes dead, damaged, diseased, and disoriented branches.

I first heard a version of the four Ds rule as a student of Orin Martin, the incomparable manager of the Alan Chadwick Garden at University of California, Santa Cruz. Start every pruning session by removing anything that is dead, damaged, diseased, or disoriented.

DEAD Cut into the branch tip and look for green, living tissue. If you don't see green, make a clean cut back to the base of the branch.

DAMAGED Broken limbs, peeling bark, or insect-damaged wood are prime candidates for removal. Diseases can enter the tree through these sites.

DISEASED Remember to disinfect between cuts. Some diseases affecting the trunk, such as gummosis on stone fruit, can be tolerated if the tree is still producing.

DISORIENTED Consider the overall tree shape, and remove misdirected branches, such as those headed straight up or back into an open center tree. If two branches cross, decide which one to keep. Remove or head back branches that jut out into pathways or that are growing at an awkward angle for fruit production.

TOOLS OF THE TRADE

Do me a favor: when you see a tool referenced in this book, pencil the word "sharp" in front of it if it isn't already there. It is true that a clean cut will tend to heal better than a rough one, but this is as important for the person making the cut as it is for the tree. As anyone who has recently upgraded his or her pruning saw will tell you, it is much more enjoyable to prune with freshly sharpened tools.

There is something very satisfying about a tool that fits your hand and the job at hand. I come from the school of thought that says, Invest in a quality tool that you like and that fits your body, and then take care of it. Allow your pruning equipment to become an extension of your body. Developing a relationship with your tools is also part of mastering a craft.

Tipping cut on a pear; notice the bud a bit behind and below the pruner blades

Your tools don't have to be color coordinated; they just need to fit your hand.

Using loppers to make a good removal cut

Degge Hays of Frog's Leap Winery finishes a three-step cut by removing this large diameter branch at the collar.

This cut into two-year-old wood and just beyond a flower bud will tend to stop growth here.

Tipping a young peach tree

Your plan for shaping your trees is tied to the tools you will be using. If you don't want to climb a ladder to prune your trees (or pick fruit), you'd better keep your trees on the small side, and that means pruning.

I have found that the implement I am holding determines the cut I will make. To be efficient in pruning, I always start with the saw or loppers and work my way down to my shears. After I finish one tree and approach a new one, I make sure that my saw is in my hand. It might seem obvious, but if I am still holding the shears I used on the last tree, I can easily get distracted and start making little clean-up cuts on a branch that actually needs to be removed entirely.

My basic pruning kit includes a small folding saw that slips easily into my back pocket, in case I decide to climb up into a larger specimen. I carry a sturdy pair of loppers that isn't too heavy but has a large enough head to remove a 2-inch diameter water sprout. My trusty garden shears feel like an extension of my arm. I also haul around a 5-foot–long fixed pole saw; the telescoping pole saws I've used didn't hold up to multiple seasons of heavy pruning.

I also bring along some combination of other tools.

- Sharpening file or stone
- Small orchard ladder
- Large pole pruner
- Marking tape to flag future cuts
- Grafting knife (useful for cleaning up rough cuts)
- A larger saw, just in case
- Twine, stakes, and weights for training
- Lath (or similar material) and a cordless circular saw for making branch spreaders
- Disinfectant spray
- Snacks, sunscreen, sunglasses, and hat
- Extra of any of these, in case a helper arrives or gets drafted into service along the way

TYPES OF CUTS

Three types of cuts are important in pruning fruit trees: removal cuts, shortening or stopping cuts, and tipping cuts.

Removal cuts are used to define the shape of your tree. These cuts should be clean, not jagged, and neither too close nor too far from the main branch. The rippled bark where the branch connects to the main trunk is loaded with cells that are very good at healing these types of wounds. Cut too close to the trunk and you can cut off too many of these cells and create a larger wound; cut too far from the trunk, and you get an ugly nub and slower healing.

Be aware that heavier branches can break off midcut, and the bark on the underside the branch can peel back all the way to the trunk, creating a wound that will not heal well. Avoid this by making a three-step cut. When removing heavy, horizontal branches (generally anything over a couple of inches in diameter), make the following series of cuts to avoid damage to the main trunk. Starting 6–12 inches past where your final cut will be, use your saw to cut from the bottom of the branch up, about a third to half of the way through the branch. An inch or two past this cut (away from the trunk and toward the tip of the branch), make a cut from the top of the branch until the weight of the branch causes the limb to fall, or until you cut all the way through. Then make your final cut just past the collar of the branch, not too close to the trunk, so that the wound will heal more easily.

Shortening or stopping cuts are made in older wood or in summer. Make these cuts when a branch has filled its allotted space or has started poking you in the arm as you walk by. These cuts are helpful in small spaces when a tree has gotten bigger than you want, and they encourage spur development and help maintain a minimum of about 6 inches of air space around each branch.

Tipping cuts are made in winter. Use these cuts into the youngest branches on the tree to encourage growth. In the case of peaches, which set fruit on new wood, many growers do a lot of tipping as a way to encouraging more new growth and fruit. Make tipping cuts at a slight angle about ¼ inch

BAD CUTS

I'd like to point out a few repeat offenders.

HACK JOBS An overzealous pruner can leave branches split, jagged, and at odd lengths. Removing more than 50 percent of a tree in a season can set fruit production and overall tree health back for years to come. If you are renewing a mature tree, take a multiple-year approach: prune a third of the growth each year for three or more years.

SPUR REMOVAL I have witnessed this problem more times than I care to remember: novice pruners "cleaning up" the branches of their fruit trees cut off the fruiting spurs. Plums, apples, pears, and many other fruit trees produce a significant amount of their crop on short fruiting spurs. These bumpy little branches might look a bit messy in winter, but you have to resist the impulse to remove these vital fruiting sites.

OUT-OF-SEASON CUTS Pruning, like fertilizing, tends to encourage growth, even in a dormant tree. Try to prune as close to bud break as possible, especially if late frosts are possible in your area. Avoid pruning citrus in fall or early winter, before the cold season hits, because any new growth will be more susceptible to frost damage. In addition, some trees, such as apricots, are so sensitive to fungal infection that you should try to prune them only in dry weather.

beyond a selected bud. Avoid making horizontal cuts or those that could collect water.

SUMMER PRUNING

Summer pruning starts in early summer, soon after the first major push of growth or as soon as you see something that is out of place on the tree. You should focus on shortening and removing the current season's growth and can continue pruning for similar reasons throughout summer. In a small home orchard, trees on semi-dwarf rootstocks can be more vigorous than space allows; summer pruning is a great tool for keeping trees small. As a tree puts on new growth and leaves, it is making an energetic investment in future returns of solar energy. By summer pruning, we remove a portion of that growth before the tree has had a chance to recoup its investment. In this way, we take tree size into our own hands and maintain a tree size that is smaller than the rootstock would normally dictate.

Summer pruning to shorten laterals on a three-year-old apple tree

This apple is being trained to a modified central leader with the help of stakes and string. That mulch looks like a soft landing spot for ripe fruit.

A stone and piece of twine
make a great training weight.

Pears can often benefit from the use of spreaders to create a more fruitful branch position.

Training Techniques

Rarely does a tree present textbook growth, and I recommend against your striving for that with too much fervor. You can, however, do a lot to help your tree develop a healthy structure by using a few simple training techniques. In many cases, you'll find these techniques to be even more effective than pruning.

SPREADERS, STAKES, WEIGHTS, AND TIES

You can make spreaders by cutting V-shaped notches into the ends of short pieces of wood. Use them to encourage wider crotch angles and better branch orientation. I keep a bucket of spreaders with me as I work, and I cut them to fit in the field.

Stakes and string can be used to pull branches into a better angle for fruit production or better growing orientation. Cut wooden stakes with a notch on one side, or use tent stakes. Pound them into the ground, attach a loop of string, and attach the loop to the tree branch and pull it into place, tying it off back at the stake. Take care not to be overly aggressive, because branches can be pulled too far, causing them to split or break off completely.

Weights and ties can be used to pull branches into a better orientation; this works best on small-diameter branches. All you need is something heavy attached to a string or wire that you hang from the branch. Make simple weights by pouring concrete into egg cartons or other reclaimed containers and setting a U-nail in the top to attach to a string or wire. Attach the weights around the middle of a branch that needs to be brought down a notch.

If you use a long stake or a more elaborate trellis structure, tying is the preferred method of training; simply attach the twine to the branch, pull it to the desired orientation, and tie it to the support. I prefer the look of natural twine over the green plastic tape that is commonly used and find it to be just as useful. Branches can also be tied to bamboo stakes to create shapes, such as fan shapes, along horizontal or vertical fence cables.

NOTCHING

Cutting a small, crescent-shaped notch just above a dormant bud can jolt the bud into life. Cutting into the cambium layer (where sap flows) under the bark of the tree blocks the growth-suppressing hormones emitted from the tree's tip and focuses sap flow coming from below at the bud just below the notch, hopefully causing it to push. Notching doesn't work every time, but it is worth a shot in your quest for a balanced tree structure or a new espalier scaffold.

Tree Shapes

Armed with a quiver of sharp tools and a firm grasp of the principles of pruning and training, your next mission is to tackle the shape of the tree. For small fruit trees not trained to a trellis or some other contorted position, two shapes are common: modified central leader and open center or vase. Perhaps another form should be included here as well: the most productive and/or pleasing shape for this tree in your space. I have seen more than one peach tree hanging great crops of fuzzy sweetness on a form that is unclassifiable.

Before I outline the specifics of each shape, I want to remind you that trees are living things, so they probably aren't going to look exactly like a diagram in a book.

Modified central leader

Open center tree form

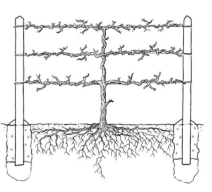

This simple espalier form has stood the test of time.

MODIFIED CENTRAL LEADER

The modified central leader shape is often used for apples, pears, cherries, and European plums. This is a great shape for a freestanding tree of moderate height. One to two tiers of branches are arranged around the main trunk, with a smaller, vase-shaped cluster around the top. Three or four lower branches are spaced about evenly up and down the main trunk or divided into whorls, with a gap of 18 inches or more between layers. The modified part of this form comes in the creation of a second whorl, or tier, of branches in a vase shape atop the main trunk.

OPEN CENTER OR VASE

This shape is usually applied to peaches, nectarines, apricots, Japanese plums, and pluots. An open center shape suits my eye so well that I sometimes find myself forcing the shape onto a tree that should really be a central leader form. To create this shape, at the time of planting, lop off the tree about knee high to encourage a low branching structure. Prune and train the next season's growth to create three to five main scaffold branches. Tip and train laterals each season to create a balanced vase shape that allows light into all parts of the tree.

ESPALIER

Apples, pears, Asian pears, and quince are often espaliered. No matter how you pronounce it, espalier is becoming a more common tree form in the American landscape, and I am glad to see it. I love the look of an established espalier. Yes, there is something a little perverse about manipulating a tree that tends to have a broad, sweeping form into a single dimension. But so what? Espalier is an adaptable form that will reward your interpretation, invention, and experimentation. And no matter how small your garden, you can fit an espaliered tree into it.

A quince trained as a fan espalier beautifully fills this custom-made trellis.

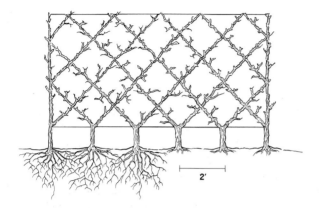

**The Belgian fence is a stunning design that
will make your neighbors envious.**

Try a number of other interesting two-dimensional tree forms. Many varieties thrive in a fan shape, with branches that radiate from the trunk. I recently planted a border for a vegetable garden in a single cordon, step-over espalier. Candelabra forms can lend a classical look to your garden. With a Belgian fence, closely spaced trees (set apart at 2 feet or less) are trained so that two braches emanate at 45-degree angles and create a woven pattern with neighboring trees. This is a great form for use as a tall screen along a driveway or side yard.

Be careful when selecting varieties for your espalier or other trellised tree form. If, for example, fireblight is an issue in your area, apples and pears can easily lose a limb each year to this bacterium, and if your tree has only six limbs, it has a lot to lose; disease-resistance becomes a very important issue.

Nurseries often bud graft fruit trees to place scaffold limbs at just the right spot to create an attractive espalier. These trees come at a premium and might or might not fit the space you are hoping to fill. If you decide to purchase one (or more) of these, get it in the ground before you set up your trellis wires, so that you can match the trellis wires to the placement of the already established branches and your planting depth.

You can establish a simple three-layer espalier without bud grafting by following a few steps.

YEAR ONE Build or choose an infrastructure (trellis or other support) where your tree(s) will grow. Select and plant bare-root trees in the dormant season. Make a nice clean cut on the main trunk, just above the bottom trellis wire or other horizontal support. If you found a tree with well-placed branches or are planting during the growing season, train branches accordingly. As new growth reaches 6 to 8 inches, use twine to train the young branches onto your trellis.

YEAR TWO Make a cut on the main trunk again, just above the second trellis wire. Remove any branches that are not part of the main structure. Continue to tie and train.

BUD GRAFTING, OR T-BUDDING

Bud grafting is a great technique for establishing espalier cordons or working with citrus, and you can do it any time the bark is slipping, or easily lifted from the wood—generally from spring to fall.

It's a relatively simple process. First, carefully remove a bud from the desired scion by starting a shallow cut about ½ inch above the bud and finishing ½ inch below. On your stock, make a cut in the shape of an inverted T, big enough to receive the little bud, and gently lift the bark and insert the bud. Next, wrap the graft with grafting tape, leaving the tip of the bud exposed. Allow two weeks for the bud to fuse, and then remove the tape and bend or notch the wood above your graft to send energy to the newly grafted bud.

NATURAL GESTURE PRUNING & TRAINING

Degge Hays finds the natural gesture of this young fig.

To illustrate that there is more than one way to prune a tree, my friend Degge Hays, garden manager at Frog's Leap Winery, has outlined his approach, which he calls natural gesture pruning.

Degge believes that fruit trees respond best when they are allowed to grow in a more natural form, with mature, finely feathered-out, fruiting branches. In natural gesture pruning, you establish a simplified central leader structure and allow the tree to express its full branch gesture, undisturbed by heading cuts. The result is a relaxed and open tree form that maximizes fruitfulness throughout the tree, minimizes sunburn, encourages balanced annual growth, and is easily maintained with less winter pruning than conventional methods.

Natural gesture pruning relies on thinning cuts and training techniques that open the tree form. Overly vigorous, misdirected, and duplicative shoots and branches are thinned, with remaining branches left unpruned. In selecting which branches to prune, consider how each branch will develop through time, imagining how the branch's own weight will bend it down into a more horizontal, and more fruitful, position, all the while exhibiting a natural grace.

I love pruning with Degge, and I like thinking about how this approach can be applied to small spaces. I like this method because it brings directly to mind the element of time and reminds me that trees are ever-changing. The longer, untipped branches take on the shape of an archer's bow, bending into to fruitful positions. I encourage you to experiment with your own pruning and explore new ideas in each season.

YEAR THREE (OR MORE) Repeat the topping cut until your tree has reached the top wire of your trellis.

ONGOING Prune your espalier in summer and winter to keep it shaped and to encourage a well-developed spur framework.

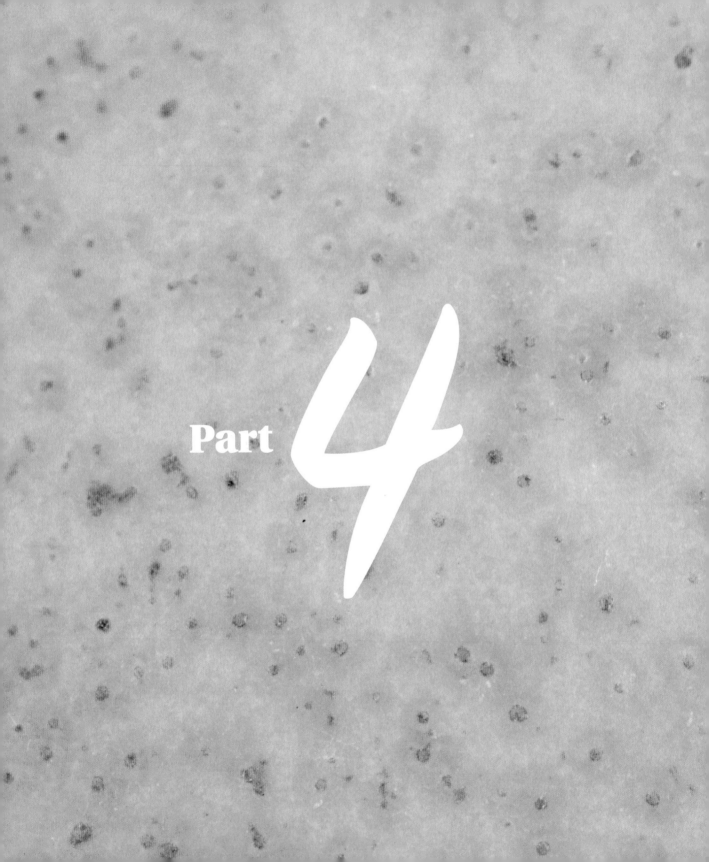

Part 4

Fruit in the Kitchen

At least five of my top ten most memorable meals have been cooked by the husband-and-wife chef team of Mike and Jenny Emanuel. I first met these guys when I moved to Napa from Berkeley and I'm sure glad I did. Mutual friends who had cooked with Mike and Jenny at Chez Panisse (Alice Waters' famous Berkeley restaurant) told us to track them down, bring our appetites, and prepare to be welcomed into their home like family. That is exactly what happened, and what has followed has been a sustaining and inspiring friendship.

Mike brings a catching enthusiasm to everything he does. He is one of those lucky people who found a way to make a profession of his passion. His passion is food, and he is clearly fed by feeding others. It is a lifetime journey that, as a gardener, I can relate to. It is the excitement that comes with knowing that I'll never master all the knowledge and skill there is to acquire within my profession. The best thing I can do is simply decide to make each day part of the journey toward mastery.

Mike's approach to cooking is simply to find quality seasonal ingredients, starting with the fruits and vegetables growing in his yard, and to draw on his vast experience and study of diverse cuisines to craft just the right dish that captures the best characteristics of those ingredients. Though he knows recipes are important, Mike relies heavily on his senses as he cooks.

Mike has, in his typical generous and enthusiastic fashion, put together some great recipes that highlight the best of seasonal homegrown fruit. Enjoy!

Poached pears are well matched with freshly whipped cream and a drizzle of the poaching juices.

A Bounty of Seasonal Fruit Recipes

by Mike Emanuel

Chef **Mike** adds just the right amount of sugar as **Colby** whips cream for the poached pears.

A collection of fruit preserves

Apricot Jam

Makes five ½-pint jars

This jam is sunshine in a jar! An all-time favorite among home preservers, apricot jam is reason alone to plant an apricot tree. Everyone loves it slathered on toast from a good country loaf, but apricot jam can be used in other ways, too: it makes an excellent glaze for fruit tarts of many kinds and is delicious spread between cake layers or spooned over scones fresh from the oven. I make thumbprint cookies with simple shortbread dough that I fill with this jam before baking. And thinned with a little wine, the jam makes a wonderful glaze for a baked ham.

I typically use about two parts fruit to one part sugar for my jams, using less sugar for sweeter fruits. Mixing together the fruit and sugar prior to cooking helps draw out the juices and fruity essence, which gives the jam a head start as heat is applied. If you're dealing with a large quantity of fruit, measure out and cook successive batches (or cook them simultaneously if you have enough pots). These small batches cook quickly, preserving the fruit's vibrant flavor and color.

Because I don't like the extra-firm texture that store-bought pectin gives my jam, I rely on the fruits' natural pectin to give my jam good, spoonable consistency. The sugar and added lemon juice are important elements of the recipe, because they help engage the fruits' thickening abilities when cooked.

3 pounds apricots, pitted, and chopped into ½-inch pieces

1 pound organic sugar, or to taste

Juice from ½ lemon, or to taste

1. Gently combine the apricots and sugar in a large nonreactive container and set aside for 2 hours or overnight in the fridge.

2. In a 225°F oven, insert a baking tray with five impeccably clean ½-pint canning jars.

3. Bring a small pot of water to a boil, turn off the heat, and drop in five new self-sealing lids (these lids are designed to seal only once). Put a dinner plate in the freezer.

4. With a rubber spatula, scrape the fruit and sugar mixture into a large, heavy nonreactive pot (copper, stainless steel, or enamel cast iron are best), or into a couple smaller heavy pots. Heat the pots containing the fruit and sugar over low heat, stirring until the sugar has completely dissolved. Bring the mixture to a boil and cook, stirring frequently to prevent scalding, for about 20 minutes, or until the large bubbles subside and smaller, thicker bubbles form.

5. Spoon a little jam onto the cold plate to check its consistency; if it is still runny and thin after sitting about 20 seconds, continue cooking the jam and check again in 5 minutes or so. When you like the consistency, turn off the heat and stir in the lemon juice. Taste and adjust. Let the jam rest for a minute or two before ladling off any scum from the top.

6. Remove the jars from the oven. Using a canning funnel, fill the jars to within ⅛ inch of the rim. Wipe any spilled jam from the rim with a clean, damp towel. Place clean lids on the jars and screw on their bands.

7. Let the jars cool to room temperature, during which time you should hear the clicking sounds of the jars sealing.

8. After the jars are cool, check the seals by pressing the lids to see if they compress or move; if a lid moves, the seal didn't take. Store those jars in the fridge for up to six months. The sealed jars keep for about a year in a dark cupboard, but they should be refrigerated after they're opened.

VARIATIONS: *Use this recipe with plums and pluots, adjusting the sugar amounts for particularly sour varieties. This recipe also works with berries.*

Peach Leaf Wine

Makes about 5 cups

This elegant almond-scented infusion is delicious when poured over sparkling wine for guests as they arrive for a dinner party, and it's also great sipped lightly chilled or on the rocks when your attitude needs realigning. Other stone fruit leaves, such as nectarine and cherry, can also be used.

Generous handful of peach leaves (about 75)

1 bottle (750ml) red wine

¾ cup vodka or brandy (80 proof)

½ cup organic sugar

1. Crush the leaves with your hands to help release their oils, and then pack them into a large, sterilized canning jar.

2. Add the remaining ingredients and stir until the sugar is dissolved. Seal the jar and store it in a cool place for about a week, shaking or stirring every few days to make sure all the sugar is dissolved.

3. Taste the wine after a week; when it's ready, it should have a pleasant bitter-almond flavor. If it's very subtle, let it go a little longer.

4. Taste again until you like the flavor. Then strain the wine through cheesecloth to remove the leaves, and pour the infused liquid into sterilized bottles. The wine is tasty just after it's been made, but the flavors truly blossom after a few months of aging.

VARIATIONS: *Add a handful of raspberries or currants to the infusion for extra flavor.*

2 pounds unblemished cherries, stem ends snipped

½ cinnamon stick

4 cloves

1-inch piece of vanilla bean

1 cup organic sugar

3 cups brandy or other spirit (80 proof)

¼ cup water

1. In two, quart-sized canning jars with narrow shoulders (they help to keep the cherries submerged), place the cherries along with the evenly divided spices and lemon zest.

2. Whisk together the sugar, brandy, and water until the sugar is dissolved; pour over the fruit.

3. Seal the jars and store in a cool place for about a month. Then refrigerate indefinitely. The flavor mellows and gets wonderfully complex over time.

OTHER CHERRY RECIPES: In his book *Ready for Dessert*, David Lebovitz candies cherries by cooking pitted cherries in sugar syrup (2 cups cherries, 1 cup sugar, 1 cup water) with a little lemon juice for about 15 minutes, or until the solution registers 220°F on a candy thermometer. They keep for six months in the fridge.

To pickle 2 pounds of cherries, boil and cool a mixture of 2 cups vinegar, 1 cup sugar, 1 cup water, 3 cloves, ¼ teaspoon black peppercorns, 2 allspice berries, 1 teaspoon mustard seeds, and 3 thin slices of fresh ginger. Pour this over cherries that have been gently packed in a sterilized container. Let the flavors blend for a few days before eating. They can be served with roasted meats and charcuterie.

Brandied Cherries

Makes about 2 quarts

This classic French country preserve can be made with a variety of dried and fresh, thin-skinned fruits. One of these beautiful spiked cherries is the ultimate garnish for a Manhattan cocktail, and served to your guests in little glasses, the brandy makes a lovely end to a dinner party. Spoon some brandied cherries over vanilla or cinnamon ice cream for a sophisticated sundae. The cherries are also classically served with charcuterie and wonderful in a salad of bitter greens, walnuts, and roasted duck or squab. Warm them in the pan juices of roast or braised pork or duck just before serving.

Any good quality brandy or other spirit, such as bourbon or rum, works well. Armagnac, an aged brandy from the south of France, is a favorite of mine.

Dried fruit comes back to life in the poaching liquids.

Dried Fruit Compote

Makes about 1½ quarts

These poached, spiced fruits are magic spooned over custard or ice cream and delicious served simply in a big bowl with lightly sweetened whipped cream and a crisp cookie. Note that this basic ratio of 4 parts liquid to 1 part sugar can be applied universally to poach any kind of dried or fresh fruit.

4 cups water

1 cup sugar, honey, or a combination

1 star anise

½ vanilla bean

2 cloves

4 peppercorns

½ cinnamon stick

2 wide strips orange rind, trimmed of white pith

2 pounds mixed dried fruit such as figs, plums, and apricots

1–2 tablespoons peach leaf wine (optional, from Peach Leaf Wine recipe)

1. Heat the water and sugar or honey in a medium sauce pan, stirring until dissolved. Add the spices and orange rind and simmer for a few minutes to allow the flavors to mingle.

2. Stir in the dried fruit, and cook at the lowest temperature for about 20 minutes, or until the fruit is tender but still retains a good texture.

3. Remove from the heat, and then stir in the optional peach leaf wine. The fruit will absorb the syrup and plump up as it sits.

4. After the fruit is cool, transfer it and the syrup to a wide-mouthed jar and refrigerate.

Little hands make apple chips magically disappear.

Apple Chips

Makes about 50 chips

You might not be surprised to find these wholesome treats garnishing a dish at a special restaurant, but they're super easy to make at home. Put out a bowl of them at your kid's birthday party and watch as the chips vanish. I've served them alongside applesauce made from the same apple variety ('Pink Pearl' is amazing), with grilled rosemary-fennel–spiced pork chops. They make a perfect garnish for any apple dessert.

2 medium-size apples

1. Heat your oven to its lowest setting, on convection mode if available.

2. On the thinnest setting of your Japanese-style mandolin slicer, slice the apples directly onto two parchment-lined baking trays. Lay the slices in a single layer, snug but not overlapping.

3. Bake the apple slices for about 45 minutes, or until they feel firm and dry; then remove them from the oven and allow to cool. After they cool completely, they will be nice and crisp.

Apple chips fresh out of the oven

Apple Galette

Makes one tart that serves six

Here's a great chance to show off your apple harvest and baking skills at the same time. Most apple varieties can be used in this recipe, but I like the richer tasting heirlooms that offer a good balance of sweet and tart flavors. Serve with vanilla ice cream or lightly sweetened whipped cream.

You can make a galette with many types of fruit, but it's important that you add sufficient flour under juicier fruit types. Because apples are relatively dry, they don't require much flour for thickening, but fruits that release a lot of juice when cooked, such as plums. peaches, and cherries, need more flour, so that juices thicken to a nice consistency and liquid doesn't leak through or over the edge of the crust.

To manage these juicy fruits, the bakers at Chez Panisse came up with an all-purpose mixture they call "moon dust," which is made of roughly equal parts almonds, sugar, and flour, pulverized in a food processor. Based on the fruit's relative juiciness, they sprinkle more or less of this mixture under the fruit while assembling the tart. I make a big batch of moon dust to store in the freezer and use throughout the season.

½ galette dough, rolled and chilled (from Galette "Crunch" Dough recipe)

1 tablespoon flour

3 pounds apples, peeled, quartered, and cored

2 tablespoons heavy cream

5 tablespoons organic sugar, or to taste

2 tablespoons apricot jam

1. Preheat the oven to 400°F.

2. Remove the rolled dough from the fridge and place it on a parchment-lined baking tray.

3. Sprinkle the flour evenly over the dough, to within about 1 inch of the edge.

4. Cut the apples into ¼-inch–thick slices. Working from the outside edges of the dough, where the flour starts, arrange the slices in a slightly overlapping pattern in a ring. Working inward, make progressively smaller rings of overlapping apples until you reach the center.

5. Fold the outer exposed dough up against the outside row of apples, pressing gently or crimping so that it stays in place.

6. Chill the assembled galette in the fridge for about 20 minutes. Remove it and brush the folded or crimped edges with cream. Evenly sprinkle sugar over the whole tart, taking care not to sprinkle it on the parchment.

7. Bake the galette on the middle rack of your oven for about 30 minutes, turning the pan a couple of times during baking, until the crust is an even, golden brown. Remove the tart from the oven, and with the help of a sturdy spatula, slide it onto a cooling rack.

8. While it cools, make the glaze: warm the jam with a little water in a small saucepan or microwave and press through a fine strainer into a small bowl.

9. Cool the galette for at least 15 minutes before glazing with the jam and slicing.

VARIATIONS: *A handful of lightly sugared huckleberries (a wild relative of the blueberry) strewn on the tart while it's baking will contribute a winey earthiness and visual appeal. Dried currants that are first plumped in a little warmed brandy also make a lovely addition. Alternating slices of poached quince with the apples makes for a unique and absolutely delicious tart.*

Apricots and pitted sweet or sour cherry galettes are the ultimate spring treat. White and yellow peaches and nectarines can be used to make classic summer tarts that I sometimes embellish with mulberries, blackberries, raspberries, or whatever the season presents. Plums and pluots can be used in stunning galettes, but they definitely require more flour mixture under the fruit and lots of sugar on top to manage their tart juiciness.

The crust on this peach galette is everything you could hope for in a rustic summer tart.

Galette "Crunch" Dough

Makes enough for 2 galettes or 1 double-crusted pie

This excellent and versatile tart and pie dough is invaluable when planning a dessert with your fruit harvest. You'll find yourself, as I do, going to this recipe throughout the year to turn your best fruit into freeform, single-crust galettes or double-crusted pies.

Beloved French chef Jacques Pèpin shared this recipe with the cooks at Chez Panisse. The technical strength of this formula lies in the two-phase incorporation of butter. The first quantity is cut into the flour fairly well, providing "shortness," or tenderness, to the baked tart. The second portion is lightly incorporated with bigger pieces left somewhat intact. These larger pieces create steam pockets during baking, which adds a flakiness to the crust. You get the best of both worlds with a tender and flaky crust!

Keeping the butter and water cold and avoiding the temptation to overwork the dough are the keys to success.

Because my hands stay warmer than your average baker, I prefer to make this dough with a standing mixer using the paddle attachment. I suggest also trying it the old-fashion way, cutting in the butter with a pastry blender or two dinner knives. This hands-on approach will give you a deeper understanding of the mechanics of this technique and ultimately make you a more skilled baker.

2 cups organic all-purpose flour

1½ teaspoons sugar

¼ teaspoon kosher salt

12 tablespoons (1½ sticks) unsalted butter, chilled and cut into ½-inch pieces

½ cup cold water

1. Combine the flour, sugar, and salt in the bowl of your standing mixer. With the paddle attachment locked in, briefly mix these to combine on the lowest speed.

2. Toss in about a third of the butter and incorporate on medium speed until the dough resembles coarse meal. Add the remaining butter and incorporate just until the bigger pieces are about the size of large peas.

3. Remove the bowl from the mixer base and drizzle the chilled water into the mass, tossing gently with your hands, letting it drop back into the bowl as you go. Keep tossing the dough until it starts to come together and is mostly free of dry patches. During this stage, don't squeeze or otherwise abuse the dough; this would over-engage the gluten in the flour, resulting in a tough crust.

4. Divide the dough in half and firmly press into two discs. Wrap each tightly in plastic and refrigerate for at least 1 hour, giving the gluten in the dough a chance to relax while the flour hydrates.

5. When you're ready to roll out the dough, remove the discs from the fridge and let them soften for a few minutes. If they've been refrigerated for several hours, they'll take longer to soften, but don't let them reach room temperature. If at any point you're concerned about the dough getting too warm, just pop it back in the fridge to rechill before you proceed.

6. Remove the plastic wrap, and on a well-floured surface, roll each disk into a 14-inch circle. Don't worry much about symmetry here; these tarts are meant to look rustic and irregular. Quickly wipe away excess flour from both sides of the dough with a soft-bristle pastry brush and carefully place the dough on a large parchment-lined baking tray. Cover with another piece of parchment and chill until you're ready to assemble the galette.

Homemade fruit leather is a far cry from the store-bought stuff.

Apple and Huckleberry Fruit Leather

Makes two large rolls

These delicious and compact fruit rolls are chockfull of big fruit energy; they are a natural for long hikes and camping trips. Plus, they have great texture, are fun to tear into, and aren't loaded with refined sugar. Because the leather is lightly sweetened and retains a lot of the fruit's natural fiber, parents can feel good giving this wholesome snack to their kids.

3 pounds apples, unpeeled, quartered, and cored

1 pound huckleberries

¼ cup sugar or honey, or to taste

Juice from 1 lemon, or to taste

1. Preheat the oven to its lowest temperature. Line two 13-by-17–inch baking trays with parchment.

2. Roughly chop the apples and put them in a large sauce pan with the berries and sugar or honey. Bring to a gentle simmer and cook until the apples are very soft, about 15 minutes.

3. Remove the fruit from the heat. Working over a bowl, pass the fruit through the finest disk of your food mill, or pulverize it in a food processor. Then press it through a fine sieve. Stir in the lemon juice and adjust the sweetness to your liking.

4. Divide the puree between the two trays and spread evenly with a spoon or a small rubber spatula.

5. Put the trays in the warm oven, and prop the door open slightly with a wooden spoon. Dry the fruit in the oven overnight or until the puree is no longer sticky. You'll know it's done when a corner lifts off the parchment freely, after about 8 hours. Let the leather cool to room temperature.

6. Slowly peel the leather free from the parchment. Cover the surface with plastic wrap, flip it over, and roll it up.

VARIATIONS: *Blackberries, blueberries, and mulberries are tasty alternatives to the huckleberries in this recipe. Any thick fruit purée can be made into leather. Plums and apricots are especially good, but know that the juiciest fruits will take the longest to dry. Add spices or other flavorings to the pot as the fruit cooks. Grated fresh ginger, for instance, is a natural with plums, and ground cinnamon with apples or pears will add a warm spice component. Try different flavorings, but add them judiciously; you want the spices to complement the fruit, not compete with or overpower it.*

'Pink Pearl' Applesauce

Makes about 1 ½ cups

Any single apple variety or combination can be used to make sauce, but I like apples with a good flavor balance of sweet and tart. The 'Pink Pearl' apple's flesh gets hot pink as it cooks. This classic applesauce pairs well with juicy slices of roast pork and crispy potato latkes, along with a dollop of crème fraiche.

4 **'Pink Pearl' apples (about 1¼ pounds), peeled, cored, and quartered**

⅓ **cup apple cider or water**

2 **tablespoons bourbon or Calvados brandy (optional)**

¼ **cup organic sugar, or to taste**

Tiny pinch salt

2 **tablespoons butter**

A few drops lemon juice

1. Place the apple peels and cores into a small saucepan and pour in the cider or water and optional liquor. Bring to a simmer and cook, covered, for about 10 minutes.

2. Slice the apples into a medium saucepan. Through a fine mesh strainer, pour the peel and core infusion over the apple slices, pressing firmly on the solids with a ladle or rubber spatula to extract as much goodness as possible.

3. Add the sugar and salt to the apples and simmer the mixture. Cover and cook gently for about 20 minutes, until the apples are very soft.

4. Toss the butter into the pan and pulverize the mixture with a potato masher to the consistency you want. Stir in the lemon juice.

Serve warm or at room temperature.

VARIATIONS: *Adding some slices of poached quince to your apples as you cook the sauce will give it a special and unique flavor. Simmer a peeled, cored, and sliced quince in syrup made from 2 cups water and ½ cup sugar with a small piece of a vanilla bean and a strip of lemon zest until tender. Then add a little of this syrup to the apples as they cook.*

In my kitchen, poaching is allowed and encouraged.

Pears Poached in Red Wine

Serves four

This lovely and honest dessert is great served with whipped cream or warm chocolate sauce. Pears that are very ripe and soft tend to get mushy when poached, so I choose those that are ripe but still firm. If you stick with a proportion of about 4 parts wine to 1 part sugar and choose firm, ripe fruit, you can successfully poach other fruits, such as peaches or apples.

1 bottle (750ml) red wine

¾ cup sugar

2 wide strips lemon zest, yellow part only

2 cloves

2-inch piece vanilla bean

4 pears (about 2 pounds), peeled, with stems attached

1. In a large saucepan, bring the wine, sugar, zest, and spices to a simmer and cook gently for a few minutes to marry flavors.

2. Slide the pears into the liquid and cook at a very gentle simmer until they offer little resistance when stabbed with a bamboo skewer. Depending on the pears' variety and ripeness, this can it can take from 15 to 45 minutes.

3. Remove the pan from the heat, let the pears cool in the syrup, and then carefully transfer the fruit to a container to store in the fridge.

To serve, remove the pears from the syrup, cut them in quarters, and with a pairing knife cut away the seeds and surrounding membrane. Or dramatically serve them whole and arm your guests with a knife and fork.

VARIATIONS: *Add huckleberries to the wine mixture to add an incredible layer of flavor to the pears. Use other spices for a more exotic dessert. You can also make a sauce by boiling down some of the poaching liquid until it thickens a little.*

Quince fruit rubbed clean of its fuzz and ready to be cut

Quince Paste

Makes one 8 × 10-inch pan

This heavenly fruit paste, or "cheese," is made extensively throughout the Mediterranean and Latin America and has recently become the darling of home preservers in the United States. It's a suave treat to serve guests as a snack with sheep's milk cheese, roasted almonds, and good dry sherry, or it can be served as small sugar-coated bites after dinner. Quince paste makes a beautiful addition to a holiday candy gift box, packed alongside your candied citrus rind and some homemade truffles flavored with brandy from your preserved cherry jar.

   Used as a savory component, a little quince paste can be melted into the pan juices from roast duck or pork cooked with bay and rosemary.

3 pounds fragrant quince, wiped of fuzz

1 lemon, cut into ¼-inch slices

2 cups organic sugar

1. Using your sharpest paring knife, quarter and core the quince fruit, being extra careful as you cut through the exceptionally tough skin and flesh. Cut the quarters into roughly ¾-inch slices, dropping them into a large, heavy pot as you go. Then add the lemon slices.

2. Add just enough water to barely cover the fruit and bring it to a simmer. Cover the pot with a piece of parchment and cook, stirring occasionally, until the quince is very soft and starting to break apart, about 30 minutes. Add more water during cooking if necessary.

3. Remove and discard the lemon slices. Pass the quince and liquid through the finest blade of a food mill into a bowl, or press through a fine mesh strainer with a rubber spatula.

4. Clean and dry the pot. Scoop the quince puree into the pot and stir in the sugar. Stirring almost constantly, cook the puree over medium heat for about 45 minutes, until it gets very thick and shiny, and mounds up somewhat. (It's smart to wear long sleeves or oven mitts as you stir to protect your arms from the molten bubbles that erupt.) If the paste starts to scorch, remove it from the heat for a few minutes before continuing.

5. Turn the paste onto a parchment-lined 8-by-10–inch baking dish that has been brushed with a little vegetable oil. Let the paste cool to room temperature, and then carefully flip it onto a fresh piece of parchment. Let it cure in a cool place for a couple days until the surface moisture has mostly dried. Cut the quince paste into slabs and wrap each in a piece of parchment. Store in the fridge.

VARIATIONS: *In* Moro: The Cookbook, *Samuel and Samantha Clark, owners of London restaurant Moro, included a recipe for a cool quince aioli they serve with lamb and pork. They pulverize quince paste with a little pounded garlic, salt, and lemon juice, and drizzle in olive oil in a food processor until it reaches a lovely consistency.*

Finished marmalade

Orange Marmalade

Makes about eight ½-pint jars

I walked into June Taylor's tranquil little shop in Berkeley, The Still Room, with a plan: to charm this master fruit preserver into teaching me how to make marmalade. Armed with a bag of uniquely fragrant 'Rangpur' limes, I was successful; my scheme worked. During that citrus season, a sweet friendship was forged as I started my journey toward understanding the nuances of making this complex preserve.

June is an international authority on fruit preserving and a cult hero in the artisan food movement. People swoon over the unusually flavored, beautifully balanced, and not-too-sweet preserves she crafts from the fruit of the area's best organic growers. This recipe is a distillation of what June has taught me and what I've discovered in my own kitchen.

Orange marmalade is famously delicious smeared on good toast or a tender buttery scone, and it's also great spread between the layers of a rich almond cake. Thin some with a little white wine or water to make a quick and delicious sweet-and-sour glaze for a baked country ham or slow-cooked pork belly. The 'Seville' orange makes classic bittersweet marmalade, but other orange varieties and virtually any citrus fruit can be used as well. I like to showcase a special citrus variety alone or combine varieties to create interesting and complex marmalades.

This recipe calls for a cotton jelly bag or cheesecloth (both of which you can find at a good kitchen supply shop). Whether you use the bag or make a pouch with the cheesecloth, the pectin rich membranes and pits you collect in this small bag will be the key to setting or jelling your marmalade.

7 pounds oranges

1 cotton jelly bag with drawstring, or 3 pieces of cheesecloth cut in 18-inch squares

⅓ cup lemon juice

9 cups water

Organic sugar

Eight half-pint canning jars, tops, and lids

Candy thermometer

1. Juice about half or up to three quarters of the oranges, pouring the juice as you go into a large, heavy, nonreactive pot. (I use a shallow and wide enamel-coated Dutch oven or a stainless steel pot.) A higher ratio of juice gives you a delicate, jellylike marmalade.

2. Put the opened jelly bag or overlapping layers of cheesecloth in a small bowl, letting the edges of cheesecloth

Fruit for marmalade

Simmer down my friends, simmer down.

hang over the side. With a spoon, scrape the membranes from each juiced half into the bag, along with the pulp and seeds that collect in the juicer. Save the excavated peel halves for a batch of candied citrus peel.

3. With a sharp knife, remove the tops and tails from the remaining oranges and cut them in half from top to bottom. With the cut sides facing up, remove the cottony pith from the center of each half by making two cuts into a V shape. Add the trimmings to the bag.

4. Cut each orange half into even wedges no more than ½-inch thick, removing any seeds and adding them to the bag. Leave these wedges whole or cut them into thirds, quarters, or smaller.

5. Scoop the fruit and any accumulated juice with a scraper or spatula into the pot as you go. Add the lemon juice and water to the pot. Securely tie up the pectin bag and toss it in the pot.

6. Bring the mixture to a simmer and cook until the rind pieces are tender and offer no resistance to the tooth when tested, 20 minutes to 1 hour. After the rind is tender, remove the pectin bag to a bowl, and place it in the fridge.

7. Measure the volume of the pot's contents, pouring it into a large bowl as you go. Based on the fruit's inherent sweetness and volume of cooked fruit, calculate a percentage of how much sugar to add. For sweeter fruit, such as navel oranges, tangerines, or 'Meyer' lemons, stir in 25 percent sugar to start until dissolved. (So, for example, if the pot ingredients measure 8 cups, you would start with 2 cups of sugar.) For marmalades based on not-so-sweet fruit, such as 'Seville' oranges or grapefruit, start with about 60 percent sugar. Taste critically for a round, sweet, and tart flavor balance, adding small increments of sugar until you like the flavor. The finished marmalade will retain this balance in concentrated form.

8. Check that the cooled pectin bag is securely tied, and squeeze it into the contents of the container, stirring in the pectin as you go; you'll need to continue squeezing it for several minutes until all the white pectin has been extracted. Discard the remaining pulp from the pectin bag.

9. Put a tray of eight, impeccably cleaned, half-pint canning jars into a 225°F oven. Have as many new, self-sealing lids (these lids are designed to seal only once) and screw-on rings handy. Put a plate in the freezer.

10. Stir the marmalade base to distribute the fruit segments, and pour some into the cleaned cooking pot, filling it no more than a third. If you have two good pots, fill them both and cook both batches at the same time. Otherwise, cook the fruit in small, successive batches. These small batches cook quickly, preserving the fruit's vibrant flavor and color. Clip on a candy thermometer and bring the marmalade to a boil and cook, stirring occasionally, for 20 to 30 minutes, until the mixture registers 220°F. To test the set, spoon a little mixture onto the chilled plate, wait about 20 seconds, and then nudge it. If it wrinkles and feels set, it's done.

11. Remove the jars from the oven. Skim away any foam from the mixture in the cooking pot with a spoon and ladle the hot marmalade into the hot jars, filling them to within ⅛-inch from the top. Wipe any spilled marmalade from the rim with a clean, damp cloth and firmly secure the lids with the screw rings.

12. Continue cooking the batches until all the mixture has been cooked and jarred.

13. After the marmalade cools, check the canning jars' seal by pressing on their tops. If the tops are firm, the seal is good. Store these in your pantry for up to a year. Unsealed jars should be stored in the fridge and will keep for six months.

VARIATIONS: Use both 'Seville' and navel oranges for a nicely balanced marmalade. One of my favorites is made from three or four fruit varieties, such as lime, grapefruit, 'Meyer' lemon, and sweet orange or tangerine.

June Taylor has trouble keeping up with demand for her 'Meyer' lemon and rosemary marmalade. Try experimenting by adding other garden herbs such as sage and thyme. Add these and other inspired flavorings to the final cooking in a clean jelly bag, removing them when their flavor is pronounced.

Vanilla bean and spirits such as rum, scotch, and bourbon are all delicious add-ins; use just enough to complement but not overwhelm the fruit.

Finished candies can be kept in a glass jar for easy access.

Candied Citrus Peel

Makes about 1 pound of candy

Making candied citrus peel (and marmalade) is a great project for a winter day. Both recipes capture the bright vibrancy of citrus. If you dedicate the good part of a weekend to cooking, you can make both marmalade and citrus peel candy. Because the recipes share similar techniques, making them together will help to reinforcing your understanding of the mechanics of cooking with citrus.

Some recipes call for a series of simmering and draining, but my preserving mentor, June Taylor, believes that you're pouring the soul of the peel down the drain each time you simmer, drain, and repeat. She and I like the edgy character of each citrus variety and suggest cutting the more intense fruit into little bites. The cream of tartar in this recipe is used to stabilize the sugar, preventing it from crystallizing when the candy is stored.

You can use grapefruit, orange, lime, or lemon rinds for this candy. Cooking time for each fruit varies, so cook only one type at a time.

About 4 pounds washed citrus fruit

Candy thermometer

4 cups water

2¼ cups unrefined sugar

½ teaspoon cream of tartar

About 2 cups white sugar

1. Top and tail the fruit so that the flesh is barely exposed, saving these "buttons" to candy with the rest. Remove the rind by scoring the fruit in wide strips, cutting down just to the flesh and then peeling away the rind. Reserve the fruit's flesh for making segments to use as the base for a marmalade batch or to eat fresh for a deluxe treat.

2. If you're working with grapefruit or oranges with very thick rinds, remove and discard some of the extraneous white, cottony pith with a spoon or paring knife.

3. Cut the peel into consistent sizes and shapes to your liking, cutting the more intense flavored fruits such as grapefruit and lime a bit smaller.

4. Fill a large, heavy stainless steel or enameled cast iron pot with water and bring to a boil. Slide in the cut peels and bring it back to a relaxed boil. Continue cooking until the peels are quite tender and offers virtually no resistance to the tooth, 20 to 45 minutes. Drain and discard the water. Wash and dry the pot.

5. With the candy thermometer clipped on the pot, combine the 4 cups of water, organic sugar, and cream of tartar in the pot and bring to a simmer, stirring with a wooden spoon to dissolve the sugar as it heats. Stir in the cooked peels and return the mixture to a simmer. Cook until the candy thermometer reads 225°F to 230°F and the peels are translucent, about 45 minutes or more. The amount of cooking time depends on the density and thickness of the peels.

6. Drain and discard the syrup and place the peels on a cooling rack set above a tray. Let them dry for a couple of days until they lose most of their tackiness. (The drying process will take longer during rainy or humid weather.)

7. Toss the peels in a big bowl with the white sugar, separating the stuck pieces as you go. Place them on a parchment-lined tray and let them dry for another two or three days. Store dry candy slices in glass jars in a cool place.

A candy thermometer is an essential piece of equipment in the fruit grower's kitchen.

The addition of a few thin slices of lemon rind dial up the tanginess of this syrup.

Citrus Leaf Syrup

Makes about 3 cups

Master fruit preserver June Taylor makes these infusions in her Berkeley production kitchen. She uses the recipe as a template to help sequester the essence of citrus or other fruit leaves brought to her by the many small farmers who grow fruit for her amazing preserves. To bolster the flavor, June sometimes adds other aromatic herbs or fruits to an infusion, staying mindful to preserve the purity of the star ingredient.

Use this versatile syrup to create a wonderfully refreshing spritzer: mix the syrup with soda water and a squeeze of citrus fruit. It also lends an intriguing aromatic note to cocktails. I like to brush it between layers of an orange or lemon chiffon cake.

2½ cups organic sugar

2 cups water

¼ teaspoon cream of tartar

Lemon leaves, picked about 75 at a time, as needed

Bottle or jar for storing

1. In a large saucepan, slowly bring the sugar, water, and cream of tartar to a boil, gently whisking to dissolve the sugar.

2. As the mixture cooks, clean any visible dirt from the leaves with a damp towel. Bruise and crush the leaves energetically with your hands for few minutes. Pack them into a canning jar and pour the boiling syrup over top. Let the syrup cool completely before loosely capping the jar.

3. After a about a week, strain the syrup into a sauce pan, pressing on the leaves with a spatula to release any clinging syrup. Discard the leaves.

4. Pick a fresh batch of leaves, and in a saucepan, bring the saved syrup to a boil. Repeat the process, letting the leaves steep for another week. Continue to repeat this process until the syrup has a bright and full taste, a total of three to five steeps.

5. Pour the completed syrup into a sterilized bottle or jar and store it in the fridge.

Sea salt and fresh ground pepper

1 tablespoon chopped mint

1 tablespoon chopped parsley

1. Roast the almonds in a 350°F oven for about 8 minutes, stirring occasionally. Watch them closely so they don't burn, and bite through a nut occasionally to check for flavor and color; when they're done, they are light brown in the center. Remove the almonds from the oven, and when they are cool, roughly chop them.

2. With a sharp paring knife, top and tail the lemon. Then cut it in half from top to bottom. With the flesh side up, cut away and discard the cottony pith from the center of both lemon halves by making a shallow V-shaped cut the length of the lemon half. Scrape away the seeds.

3. Cut each half into several small wedges. Cut the wedges into thin slices, adding them to a bowl along with any accumulated juices.

4. With a microplane grater or mortar and pestle, process or smash the garlic into a paste and add it to the chopped lemon along with the remaining ingredients. Taste and adjust the seasonings.

'Meyer' Lemon and Roasted Almond Relish

Makes about 1 cup

'Meyer' lemons' aromatic zest, mild rind, and sweet-tart flesh make them perfectly suited for this quick relish. I embrace any chance to use the whole fruit—that's what makes this condiment unique. The rich flavor and texture of roasted almonds creates a great contrast to the lemon's brightness. This relish complements fish, chicken, and vegetables cooked on the grill.

¼ **cup raw almonds**

1 small 'Meyer' lemon

1 garlic clove, peeled

⅓ **cup good olive oil**

VARIATIONS: Try using other citrus, such as kumquats or 'Rangpur' limes. Substitute hazelnuts or other nuts for the almonds. Chopped green olives in place of the nuts make another great relish. Chives or finely chopped thyme can also be used in place of the listed herbs.

To expand the citrus flavors, I like to wrap pieces of fish in several leaves from the lemon tree before grilling them. I gently secure the bundle with a couple loops of kitchen twine. Use leaves from a fig tree and you will be rewarded with an incredible flavor similar to toasted coconut. This works with a large fish fillet or a medium-size whole fish. Once cooked and unwrapped, the charred leaves look rustic and beautiful served under the fish.

Orange wine on ice

Orange Wine

Makes a generous 5 liters (six standard wine bottles)

I was part of a small group of cooks at Chez Panisse who made this delicious aperitif each winter to pour at summer's first heat spike. The pleasant astringency balanced with sugar, spices, and not a small dose of spirits makes this a perfect grown-up refreshment. We like it poured over ice with a twist, but it also finds its way into spontaneous cocktails with gin or vodka and in dry sparkling wines for a modern spin on the mimosa.

'Seville' oranges are the classic choice for this French country cordial. Vanilla's warm aroma helps balance the high-tone flavors of this citrus fruit.

The brief dunk in boiling water kills bacteria on the fruit surface, making the infusion more stable. To keep your preserving adventures safe and stable, all your equipment and containers must be impeccably clean and storage jars sterilized in boiling water before you get started.

Large ceramic or glass crock

2 pounds 'Seville' oranges

1 navel or blood orange

2 'Meyer' (or standard) lemons

6 bottles (750ml each) crisp white or rose wine (avoid heavily oaked wines)

3 cups sugar

3 cups vodka

½ vanilla bean

1. Working in batches, if necessary, blanch the fruit in a large pot of boiling water for 30 seconds. Let the fruit dry in a colander and refresh under cold water.

2. Cut each fruit in half and juice them all. Pour the juice through wire strainer into a meticulously washed crock, pushing firmly on the pulp to extract all the juice. Discard the seeds. Add the juiced citrus cups (the peel and contents after juicing) to the container along with the other ingredients. Stir well for 2 or 3 minutes to dissolve the sugar. Cover the container and store in a cool place. Save and sterilize the empty wine bottles to refill with orange wine.

3. Taste the infusion after a couple weeks to test the flavor, and continue to do this until you like the flavor. It's ready, usually in about three weeks, when it offers a nice balance of sweet fruit with some tartness and pleasant bitterness.

4. When you like the flavor, strain the infusion through a fine mesh strainer into an impeccably clean container. Discard the solids. Let the liquid sit undisturbed for a day to allow the sediment to settle.

5. Using a food-grade siphon hose to transfer the liquid, strain the wine through a strainer lined with several layers of cheesecloth into another clean container.

6. Bottle the wine in the sterilized bottles, and cork each tightly. Store the filled bottles in the fridge for about a year, pulling out the wine to enjoy whenever you get overheated.

VARIATIONS: Good citrus alternatives include grapefruits, 'Rangpur' limes, navel or blood oranges, or a combination of citrus fruits. The cocktail grapefruit is a great choice. This pommelo-mandarin hybrid is very juicy with a lovely sweet flavor balanced with a nice amount of grapefruit verve. These qualities are released in the infusion. Our friend Anne made a batch with 'Rangpur' lime that really rocks. The fruit's zest is incredibly aromatic and the flesh is quite sour, elements that make for an ideal aperitif.

Experiment with adding other spices you like, such as peppercorns, cloves, or star anise, but don't let them overpower the citrus. I sometimes add a little red wine in with the white, lending a lovely pink hue to the infusion.

'Meyer' lemons ready to be covered with juice and put up

Preserved Lemons

Makes about 11 cups,
or two 2-quart canning jars

Preserved lemons are a delicious kitchen staple, and their uses seem endless. They are an essential condiment used to flavor many of Morocco's wonderfully fragrant stews, vegetable dishes, and salads. The preserved lemon rind and juice add an incomparable flavor sparkle to any dish. Try adding a splash of the juice to your bloody Mary, or use it to liven up a salad dressing. Marinate olives with preserved lemon for a classic Moroccan snack.

These vividly flavored lemon pickles get their character from some great spices and a naturally occurring fermentation process that thrives in the salt-rich and fruity environment. Keeping the jars sealed and at room temperature during ripening is important for the friendly bacteria to thrive, which in turn transforms these lemons into a deliciously complex and healthy condiment.

As a visual salve for the winter blues, preserved lemons shout "sunshine!" while perched on your kitchen counter, and the daily shaking of the jar keeps you engaged with the month-long fermentation process. Many recipes call for salt and lemons only, which makes excellent pickles, but the additional spices in this recipe help connect it to its North African roots.

About 40 (8 pounds, or more as needed), 'Meyer' lemons (or a combination of varieties)

1 tablespoon whole coriander seed

1½ cups kosher or fine sea salt

2, 2-quart canning jars, meticulously washed

½ teaspoon black peppercorns

2 cinnamon sticks

4 bay leaves (European style)

4 cloves

1. Juice about half the lemons to generate 3 cups of juice, reserving the juiced halves for a batch of candied peel (see pages 234–235.) Wipe the remaining lemons with a damp, clean cloth to remove any dirt.

2. With a mortar and pestle (or improvise using a clean, smooth stone in a wooden bowl), coarsely grind the coriander with a teaspoon of the salt. Add the rest of the salt to the coriander mixture and spoon 1 tablespoon into the bottom of each quart jar.

3. Cut each lemon into quarters, keeping the fruit connected at the end by stopping your cut ½ inch from the bottom. Toss them into a large bowl as you go.

4. Working over the bowl, open each cut lemon and season the exposed flesh generously with the coriander salt. It's important that you use up all the salt mixture in this step.

5. Reshape the lemons and pack them evenly into the jars, adding the remaining spices between the layers in both jars. Press the fruit down firmly as you go, to extract as much juice as they will weep.

6. Scrape any salt mixture left behind into the jars and again press down on the lemons. Add enough fresh-squeezed juice to cover the fruit, juicing more lemons if needed.

7. Seal the jars and let them sit at room temperature. Gently shake the jars daily to keep the salt and juice well distributed. If the lemons at the top do not stay submerged, open the jars and press them down; then quickly reseal. Keeping oxygen out of the jars helps the fermentation process move along.

These unique pickles are ready to eat in about a month, after which time, they should be stored in the fridge. They start to lose their brightness after a year, just in time to start a fresh batch. To use your lemon pickles, scrape away and discard the pulp and rinse the rinds well before using them and their juice in recipes.

VARIATIONS: *I like to combine different lemon varieties, capturing the distinctive qualities of each and making for more a complex flavor. It's also worth trying other tart citrus fruit such as the 'Rangpur' lime in place of or together with the lemons.*

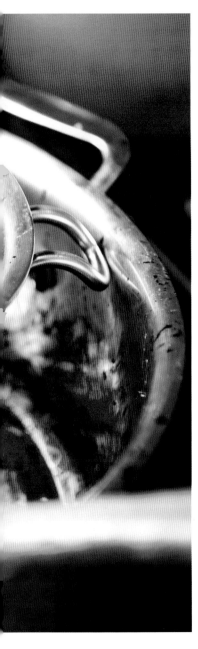

Ready for cleanup

Resources

U.S. ORGANIZATIONS

California Rare Fruit Growers (CRFG)
The Fullerton Arboretum, CSUF
PO Box 6850
Fullerton, California 92834
www.crfg.org
Good source for information about
unusual fruit trees

**Cornell University Cooperative
Extension**
http://cce.cornell.edu/Ag/Pages/
default.aspx
Information about agriculture,
gardening, and sustainability

Home Orchard Society
PO Box 230192
Tigard, Oregon 97281-0192
www.homeorchardsociety.org
Nonprofit education organization
devoted to home orchards

Midwest Fruit Explores (MIDFEX)
PO Box 93
Markham, Illinois 60428-0093
www.midfex.org
Information for home fruit growers in
the Midwest

**National Center for Home Food
Preservation**
www.uga.edu/nchfp/
Information, including publications, on
techniques for on canning and
preserving food

**North American Fruit Explorers
(NAFEX)**
1716 Apples Road
Chapin, Illinois 62628
www.nafex.org
Information about growing fruit trees

USDA Cooperative Extension Offices
www.csrees.usda.gov/Extension
Find the nearest Cooperative Extension
office

U.S. PLANT SOURCES

Cummins Nursery
1408 Trumansburge Road
Ithaca, New York 14850
607-227-6147
www.cumminsnursery.com
Custom-grown apples, pears, cherries,
and plums

Dave Wilson Nursery
800-654-5854
www.davewilson.com
Resource for home fruit tree growers

Four Winds Growers
887-449-4637, Ext. 1
www.fourwindsgrowers.com
Resource for citrus growers

Nature Hills Nursery
9910 North 48th Street, Suite 200
Omaha, Nebraska 68134-2548
888-864-7663
www.naturehills.com
Fruit trees for home gardeners

Raintree Nursery
391 Butts Road
Morton, Washington 98356
800-391-8892
www.raintreenursery.com
Resource for fruit and nut trees; good
information for home gardeners in the
Pacific Northwest

Seeds of Change
888-762-7333
www.seedsofchange.com
Organically grown apple trees

Trees of Antiquity
20 Wellsona Road
Paso Robles, California 93446
805-467-9909
www.treesofantiquity.com
Heirloom fruit trees for home gardens

Willis Orchard Company
PO Box 119
Berlin, Georgia 31722
866-586-6283
www.willisorchards.com
Fruit tree growers

CANADIAN ORGANIZATIONS

Atlantic Canada Master Gardeners Association
www.atlanticmastergardeners.com
Eastern Canada resource with links to local clubs and events and blogs, plus answers to garden questions

Master Gardeners Association of British Columbia
5251 Oak Street
Vancouver, British Columbia V6M 4H1
604-257-8662
www.bcmastergardeners.org
Newsletters, tips, photos, and links to public gardens, nurseries, and seed sources; garden organizations; and botanical references

Master Gardeners of Ontario Inc.
www.mgoi.ca
Advice, information, and links to groups, public gardens, plant societies, and resources

Toronto Botanical Garden
416-397-1345
www.torontobotanicalgarden.ca/
mastergardener/newforum
Links to fact sheets and "Ask a Master Gardener" gardening forum

University of Saskatchewan Master Gardener Program
ccde.usask.ca/mastergardener

CANADIAN PLANT SOURCES

Derry's Orchard & Nursery
www.derrysorchardandnursery.ca
604-856-9316
Specializes in apple growing in southern British Columbia. Good source for apple scion wood and fruit tree rootstocks, dwarf trees, information on tree care, mason bee condos, and llama manure.

Grimo Nut Nursery
979 Lakeshore Road, RR 3
Niagara-On-The-Lake, Ontario L0S 1J0
905-934-6887
www.grimonut.com
Primarily nut trees, but also some fruit trees, including relatively rare ones

Hortico Nurseries Inc.
422 Concession 5 East
Waterdown, Ontario L0R 2H1
905-689-6984
www.Hortico.com
Commercial nursery source that includes fruit trees; worldwide shipping

Rhora's Nut Farm and Nursery
33083 Wills Road, RR 1
Wainfleet, Ontario L0S 1V0
905-899-3508
www.nuttrees.com
Limited fruit trees, but some unusual ones offered here

Siloam Orchards
7300 3RD Concession
Uxbridge, Ontario L9P 1R1
905-852-9418
www.siloamorchards.com
Heirloom and other apple, pear, plum, cherry, and hardy peach trees

CANADIAN PUBLIC GARDENS

City of Calgary Public Orchards
http://content.calgary.ca/CCA/
City+Hall/Business+Units/Parks/
Get+involved/Community+orchards/
Community+orchards.htm
Information on the public orchard sites in Calgary

University of British Columbia Botanical Garden
6804 Southwest Marine Drive
Vancouver, British Columbia V6T 1Z4
604-822-3928
www.botanicalgarden.ubc.ca
Seventy acres of garden includes a food garden with seasonal vegetables surrounded by espaliered apple and pear trees.

Conversion Tables

Measures

INCHES	CM
¼	0.6
⅓	0.8
½	1.3
¾	1.9
1	2.5
2	5.1
3	7.6
4	10
5	13
6	15
7	18
8	20
9	23
10	25
20	51
30	76

FEET	M
1	0.3
2	0.6
3	0.9
4	1.2
5	1.5
6	1.8
7	2.1
8	2.4
9	2.7
10	3
20	6
30	9
40	12
50	15
60	18
70	21
80	24
90	27
100	30

Cooking measures

U.S.	METRIC
1 teaspoon	5 ml
1 tablespoon	15 ml
¼ cup	59 ml
½ cup	118 ml
¾ cup	177 ml
1 cup	237 ml
1 pint	473 ml
1 quart	0.95 liter
1 gallon	3.79 liter

Temperatures

°F	°C
−15	−26
20	−7
32	0
40	4
45	7
60	16
65	18
220	104
225	107
230	110
350	177
400	204

To convert temperatures
$°C = 5/9 \times (°F - 32)$
$°F = (9/5 \times °C) + 32$

Further Reading

Bender, Steve, ed. 2004. *The Southern Living Garden Book.* Birmingham, Alabama: Oxmoor House.

Blodgett, Bonnie, et al. 2004. *Midwest Top 10 Garden Guide.* Menlo Park, California: Sunset Publishing Corporation. Guide to growing favorite plants, including fruit, in Illinois, Indiana, Iowa, Kansas, Michigan, Minnesota, Missouri, Nebraska, North Dakota, South Dakota, Ohio, Wisconsin, Saskatchewan, Manitoba, and Ontario.

Bowden, Robert E., et al. 2006. *Florida Top 10 Garden Guide.* Menlo Park, California: Sunset Publishing Corporation. Guide to how to grow favorite Florida plants, including fruits.

Brown, George E. 2004. *The Pruning of Trees, Shrubs and Conifers.* 2nd ed. Revised and expanded by Tony Kirkham. Portland, Oregon: Timber Press.

Clark, Samuel and Samantha. 2011. *Moro: The Cookbook.* London: Ebury Press.

Creasy, Rosalind. 2010. *Edible Landscaping.* 2nd ed. San Francisco: Sierra Club Books. Revision of an essential reference for designing and growing an edible garden.

Dave Wilson Nursery. 2010. *What Is Backyard Orchard Culture?* www.davewilson.com/homegrown/BOC_explained.html. Accessed 4 May, 2012.

Denzer, Kiko. 2007. *Build Your Own Earth Oven: A Low-cost, Wood-fired Mud Oven.* Blodgett, Oregon: Handprint Press.

Diacono, Mark. 2010. *The Food Lover's Garden: Amazing Edibles You Will Love to Grow and Eat.* Portland, Oregon: Timber Press.

Gilsenan, Fiona, et al. 2005. *Northwest Top 10 Garden Guide.* Menlo Park, California: Sunset Publishing Corporation.

Lebovitz, David. 2010. *Ready for Dessert.* Berkeley, California: Ten Speed Press.

Lowenfels, Jeff, and Wayne Lewis. 2010. *Teaming with Microbes: The Organic Gardener's Guide to the Soil Food Web.* Rev. ed. Portland, Oregon: Timber Press.

MacCasky, Mike, Lynn Ocone, et al. 2005. *Tri-State Top 10 Garden Guide.* Menlo Park, California: Sunset Publishing Corporation. Guide to growing favorite plants, including fruits, in New York, New Jersey, and Connecticut.

Olkowski, William, Sheila Daar, and Helga Olkowski. 1991. *Common-Sense Pest Control: The Least Toxic Solutions for Your Home, Garden, Pets, and Community.* Newton, Connecticut: Taunton Press.

Ortho Books. 2004. *Complete Guide to Vegetables, Fruits & Herbs.* Des Moines, Iowa: Meredith Corporation.

———. 2004. *Home Gardeners Problem Solver: Symptoms and Solutions for More than 1,500 Garden Pests and Plant Ailments.* 3rd ed. Des Moines, Iowa: Meredith Corporation.

———. 2008. *All About Citrus & Subtropical Fruits.* Des Moines, Iowa: Meredith Corporation. Thorough guide to growing a wide range of subtropical plants.

Otto, Stella. 1993. *The BackYard Orchardist: A Complete Guide to Growing Fruit Trees in the Home Garden.* Maple City, Michigan: OttoGraphics.

Page, Martin. 2008. *Growing Citrus: The Essential Gardener's Guide.* Portland, Oregon: Timber Press.

Pollan, Michael. 2001. *Botany of Desire: A Plant's-eye View of the World*. New York: Random House.

Reich, Lee. 2008. *Uncommon Fruits for Every Garden*. Portland, Oregon: Timber Press.

———. 2009. *Landscaping with Fruit*. North Adams, Massachusetts: Storey Publishing. Thorough look at growing most fruits in your garden.

Schneider, Elizabeth. 1990. *Uncommon Fruits & Vegetables: A Commonsense Guide*. New York: William Morrow & Co. A guide to lesser-known fruits and vegetables, including selection and care.

Soler, Ivette. 2011. *The Edible Front Yard: Creating Curb Appeal with Fruits, Flowers, Vegetables, and Herbs*. Portland, Oregon: Timber Press.

Sunset Books. 1996. *Citrus*. Menlo Park, California: Sunset Publishing Corporation. Thorough look at growing citrus in home gardens and containers.

———. 1997. *National Garden Book*. Menlo Park, California: Sunset Publishing Corporation. General reference guide to more than 6000 plants, with detailed climate zone descriptions for the entire United States and parts of Canada.

———. 1998. *Western Garden Problem Solver*. Menlo Park, California: Sunset Publishing Corporation. Companion to the Western Garden Book; guide to controlling pests, diseases, and cultural problems.

———. 2004. *California Top 10 Garden Guide*. Menlo Park, California: Sunset Publishing Corporation.

———. 2005. *The Edible Garden*. Menlo Park, California: Sunset Publishing Corporation. Guide to designing and growing an edible garden.

———. 2007. *Western Garden Book*. 8th Ed. Menlo Park, California: Sunset Publishing Corporation. Comprehensive reference guide known as the bible of West Coast gardening.

———. 2010. *Western Garden Book of Edibles: The Complete A to Z Guide to growing Your Own Vegetables, Herbs, and Fruits*. Menlo Park, California: Sunset Publishing Corporation. Complete, easy-to-navigate reference guide for Western gardeners.

Photo Credits

Anaja Creatif, ©iStockphoto.com: page 237.

Anne Kitzman Photography, ©iStockphoto.com: page 152.

Aya Brackett: page 45 bottom right.

Cathleen Abers-Kimball, ©iStockphoto.com: page 117 left.

Colby Eierman: pages 40, 60, 66, 69 top, 183 top, 193 bottom.

David Smith Photography, ©iStockphoto.com: page 228.

John Panella, ©depositphotos: page 151.

Kevin Miller, ©iStockphoto.com: page 119 left.

Kevin Sesko, ©iStockphoto.com: page 120 right.

Marci Hunt LeBrun: pages 1, 2, 6, 20, 21, 52, 53, 172, 173, 212, 213.

Mark Sauerwein, ©iStockphoto.com: page 120 left.

Marko Plevnjak, ©iStockphoto.com: page 221.

Michael Tomlinson, Dave Wilson Nursery: pages 45 bottom left, 57, 71 left and right, 72 left and right, 73 left, 74 left and right, 78, 79 left and right, 80 left, 81 right, 86, 87 left and right, 88 left, middle, and right, 91, 92 left and right, 93 right, 100, 101 left and right, 102 left and right, 103 left and right, 113, 114 left and right, 115 left, middle, and right, 118 right, 121 right, 122, 123, 129 right, 131 left and right, 132 left and right, 133, 137 left, middle, and right, 188.

Murphy_Shewchuk, ©iStockphoto.com: page 116 right.

Nicole Branan, ©iStockphoto.com: page 224.

Pattiann Koury: pages 183 bottom, 186, 232 top and bottom.

Roger Whiteway, ©iStockphoto.com: page 85.

Ron Ludekens, CreatorsPalette.com: pages 70, 73 right, 83, 93 left, 94, 117 right.

Start Bro's Nurseries & Orchards Co.: page 129 left.

Terry J Alcorn Inc., ©iStockphoto.com: page 162.

Tom Gowanlock, ©iStockphoto.com: page 156 left.

Trees of Antiquity: pages 80 right, 81 left, 119 right, 121 left, 127, 128 right, 130 left and right, 136.

UC-Riverside Citrus Variety Collection: pages 145, 147 right, 148 right, 150 left, 153 left, 155 left, 163, 164, 165 left, 167, 168 right, 170, 171.

University of Minnesota, David L. Hansen: pages 116 left, 118 left.

All other photos by Erin Kunkel.

Illustration Credits

Joel Holland, pages 39, 47–49, 178 left

Marjorie Leggitt, pages 177, 178 right, 208, 210

Index

About the Author

Colby Eierman is a landscape designer and consultant who plants fruit trees and other tasty things primarily in Napa and Sonoma counties in California. He has served as the director of sustainable agriculture for Benziger Family Winery in Sonoma, where he oversaw the fruit, vegetable, and livestock programs for this industry-leading biodynamic estate. He also spent four years as director of gardens for COPIA: The American Center for Wine, Food and the Arts, in Napa. Eierman received his bachelor's of Landscape Architecture from the University of Oregon and a certificate in Ecological Horticulture from the University of California, Santa Cruz. For the past decade, Colby has maintained a consulting and design business focused on creating beautiful spaces that produce good things to eat. In that time, he has also grown fruits and vegetables for such distinguished restaurants as Chez Panisse (Berkeley, California), Roxanne's (Larkspur, California), El Dorado Kitchen, and Girl and the Fig (both Sonoma, California). As an advocate for kids' gardening programs, he cofounded the School Garden Project in Eugene, Oregon.